the nativity story

the nativity story

Contemplating Mary's Journeys of Faith

Edited by Rose Pacatte, FSP

Pauline

BOOKS & MEDIA

Boston

Library of Congress Cataloging-in-Publication Data

The Nativity story : contemplating Mary's journeys of faith / edited by Rose Pacatte.

   p. cm.

  ISBN 0-8198-5164-7 (pbk.)

   1. Mary, Blessed Virgin, Saint—Meditations. 2. Jesus Christ—Nativity. 3. Nativity story (Motion picture) 4. Christian women—Religious life. I. Pacatte, Rose.

  BT608.5.N38 2006

  232.91—dc22

2006030511

The Scripture quotations contained herein are from the *New Revised Standard Version Bible: Catholic Edition*, copyright © 1989, 1993, Division of Christian Education of the National Council of the Churches of Christ in the United States of America. Used by permission. All rights reserved.

Cover design by Rosana Usselmann

"the nativity story" © MMVI New Line Productions, Inc. Quotations from "the nativity story" appear under license from New Line Productions, Inc.

Photographs by Jaimie Trueblood. All photographs © MMVI New Line Productions, Inc.

Published by Pauline Books & Media, 50 Saint Paul's Avenue, Boston, MA 02130-3491. www.pauline.org.

Printed in the U.S.A.

Pauline Books & Media is the publishing house of the Daughters of St. Paul, an international congregation of women religious serving the Church with the communications media.

1 2 3 4 5 6 7 8 9   11 10 09 08 07 06

To our mother, Mary

Contents

Introduction

In May 2006 I was invited to read the script for a film being produced by New Line Cinema called *The Nativity Story*. Following that, I was invited to join a group of Christian journalists from various Catholic and Protestant outlets who were planning to visit the movie set in Italy during production. It turned out to be a memorable experience in many respects. It was a wonderful opportunity to observe firsthand how a major motion picture is actually made. In addition, we were able to interview the screenwriter, Mike Rich (*Finding Forrester, The Rookie, Radio*); the Oscar- and Golden Globe-nominated director, Catherine Hardwicke (*Thirteen, The Lords of Dogtown*); the producers, Marty Bowen and Wyck Godfrey; and also the lead actors: in the role of Mary, Oscar- and Golden-Globe nominee Keisha Castle-Hughes (*Whale Rider, Star Wars: Episode III—Revenge of the Sith*), and in his first major motion picture, playing the role of Joseph, Julliard-trained stage actor Oscar Issac. Their combined talent and reverence for telling the story of the year before Jesus' birth signaled to all of us that the release of *The Nativity Story* would be a major theatrical event for all audiences— and especially for the Christian faith community.

The Nativity Story is a unique blending of the Gospel infancy narratives of Matthew and Luke. The film

renders these accounts into a beautiful cinematic imagining of Mary's life from the year or so before Jesus'
birth right through to the escape of Joseph, Mary, and
the Child Jesus into Egypt. Screenwriter Mike Rich
loves to tell stories about ordinary people who do
extraordinary things. Far from being a one-dimension-
al tableau, Rich's script lets us see inside the story's characters so we can know them and feel what they might
have felt in the face of the momentous experience of the
incarnation and birth of Jesus.

There are many compelling sequences in *The
Nativity Story,* but a few stand out in my mind. One is a
touching scene in which Mary, who in a single day has
gone from girlhood to being an expectant mother and is
frightened of what this will mean, greets her older,
wiser cousin Elizabeth. Another is when Joseph tells
Mary that, because an angel visited him in a dream, he
believes the child growing within her is from God and
will save the people from their sins. Yet another is the
marvelous scene in which the poorest of the poor, the
shepherds in the vicinity of Bethlehem, find out that, on
this night, God indeed is fulfilling the hope within
them—and all people. I believe that *The Nativity Story*
will assure every child who will ever have a part in a
Christmas play that no role in this story is insignificant!

The Catholic French film critic André Bazin believed that many films, whether explicitly religious or
those dealing with some question of faith, are examples

of cinematic art as religious experience. *The Nativity Story* expresses both art and religion, and the miracle of God-become-man is incarnated again for us through the medium of film.

Director Catherine Hardwicke began her career as an architect, art director, and production designer; she ensured that the movie sets for *The Nativity Story* were authentic recreations based on first-century literary sources and archaeology. She also wanted the film shot in 35mm wide screen format with many close-ups, a style of filming that created a kind of epic intimacy between the audience and the biblical characters, especially Mary, Joseph, Elizabeth, Joaquim, Anna, the magi, and the shepherds.

"The reason I agreed to direct *The Nativity Story*," explains Hardwicke, "is because of the way the screenwriter, Mike Rich, got inside the heart and soul of the characters, and inside this kind of miracle that happened so long ago. How do you get inside a leap of faith? I wanted to do that."

Both the producer, Mary Bowen, and the screenwriter, Mike Rich, acknowledge the influence of Mel Gibson's 2005 *The Passion of the Christ* on the writing and making of *The Nativity Story*. Bowen saw Gibson's film as a demonstration that it is possible to make a biblical film that will attract audiences. Mike Rich felt moved by Gibson's portrayal Mary. "I was really inspired by the scene where Jesus falls while carrying the cross and Mary has a flashback to Jesus as a small child in danger and feels her maternal instinct kick in to save him. I felt that was completely true to their relationship; this Mary was *believable.* I knew then that I wanted to risk taking a speculative approach to developing the characters of Mary, Joseph, Anna, Joaquim, and Elizabeth."

Seeing *The Nativity Story,* reading versions of the script, visiting the set and meeting the principle filmmakers and actors—these experiences have been an inner journey for me as well. Mary was an ordinary person who did the most extraordinary thing possible: she became the mother of God—without losing any of her authenticity as a human being. *The Nativity Story* unfolds naturally, giving us a Mary who is real and accessible—and yet who believes in the impossible. This kind of Mary speaks to everyone. The Virgin Mary belonged—and belongs—totally to God, yet she lived with her husband, Joseph, who gave her the protection of his name and a father for her son. Mary is friend, neighbor, daughter, cousin—and sister to us all.

During lunch one day on the movie set, Keisha Castle-Hughes was talking about her experience playing Mary. "I told myself, 'I can't believe I'm playing this part.' We don't really know a lot about these people: who they were or what they looked like; and yet we have to *become* them now for people all over the world. You never think about it, but Mary was thirteen when she had a child. I mean, she was just a girl, playing with her friends, and then suddenly she has this huge responsibility...to become mother of the world!"

Like Keisha, I think about Mary differently now. Before, Mary was an apparition in a white gown with a blue sash; now, because of the film, I see her as a woman—human like us—who listened to that "still small voice" within her and responded to God's invitation and grace with a grace of her own. Mary was a human being, like us. She experienced life fully and within the context of her culture, the time and place where she lived; she responded to God's word in the Scriptures, as we do. But then she responded to God's unique invitation to be the mother of his Son, and our mother, too. She really is mother of the world.

In *The Nativity Story,* "journey" is a constant theme. Throughout the year before Jesus' birth, Mary was a woman "on the move," a woman on a journey of remarkable faith in God. Some of Mary's journeys were spiritual, beginning and ending within Mary's heart and soul. Others were physical, requiring her to move from place to place. But whether spiritual or physical, they were *her* journeys to make. And through her journeys, she shows us how to live our journeys, too.

In this wonderfully diverse volume, women of different ages, ethnic backgrounds, cultures, and experiences reflect on their own "journeys of faith." Some are married, some have children and grandchildren, others are widows, and still others are women religious. The authors share with us the meaning they have gleaned from Mary's journeys and example, both as recounted in the Scriptures and in the honor the Church has offered her through the centuries. They bring with them a rich and varied spiritual heritage of Marian spirituality and a willingness to share openly the role Mary plays in their lives.

As you continue your own spiritual journeys through life, join us through the pages of this book: *The Nativity Story: Contemplating Mary's Journeys of Faith.*

SR. ROSE PACATTE, FSP,
Editor

CHAPTER 1

Mary's Journey of Everyday Life

Dr. Mayra Fernandez was born in the Dominican Republic. By the time she was eight, she had moved with her family to New York after living for four years in Cuba. She attended Catholic boarding schools in New Jersey and Canada. Fernandez received her doctorate in multicultural education from the University of San Francisco in California and has written several books including *The Gospel According to Maria*. You may contact her at info@drmayrafernandez.com or go to:
www.drmayrafernandez.com.

The Virgin's name was Mary.

LUKE 1:27

❦

THE POET ASKS, "WHAT'S IN A NAME? A rose by any other name would smell as sweet" (Shakespeare's *Romeo and Juliet*). Mary, the mother of Jesus, was most likely named after Miriam, the prophetess of the Old Testament. Miriam was Moses' sister who, as a young girl, saved him from death by doing as her mother told her: placing him in a waterproof basket and hiding him in the reeds along the Nile River. Pharaoh was killing off all Hebrew boys because the Jewish people had become too numerous and potentially powerful. When Pharaoh's daughter "found" the baby in the river, Miriam boldly claimed, "I know someone who can nurse him...." That someone was the baby's own mother (see Ex 1, 2:1–10). By saving Moses, Miriam became the instrument for saving God's Chosen People. Without Miriam's courageous "yes" to her mother, there would not have been a Moses who grew up to lead his people. Certainly, Anna and Joaquim knew the story of Miriam—in Egyptian the name means love— when they gave their precious little girl the same name. There *is* something in a name!

Like Miriam of the Hebrew Scriptures, Mary of Nazareth also spoke to save others—us—and her words, too, were more than mere talk. "Yes," the language of love of God, was for Mary a language of action. At the Annunciation Mary said, "... let it be with me according to your word" (Lk 1:38). She *accepted.* At Cana: "They have no wine," and then, "Do whatever he tells you" (Jn 2:3, 5). She *prodded.* Having responded to Jesus throughout his life, Mary stood with him through his agony (see Jn 19:25). She *accompanied.* Love and action go together.

The Mary that we see and hear in *The Nativity Story,* as well as the biblical Mary we read about in the Gospels, is quite a role model for all of us. She was full of loving action and oh-so-real! This Mary doubted, cried, hurt. She helped her family make and distribute goat cheese; although not her favorite pastime, she did it because working to help her family was the right thing to do. She had fun with her friends, and she helped fill another woman's jug with water. Even as a teenager, she shows us how to do the right thing, despite how difficult this might be. Can you imagine Mary looking at the angel, shrugging her shoulders, and mumbling "whatever"?

As imagined in one powerful scene in *The Nativity Story,* Mary was also a girl who could not swim. Because her village lay in a geographic basin surrounded by limestone hills, its only water source was a well fed by a spring. I was instantly delighted: Yes, this girl was indeed someone I could commiserate with. Growing up in New York City's barrio, most of us kids had only fire hydrants to cool us off during the summer. We didn't have the opportunity to learn to swim either, and this insight gave me yet another connection to Mary.

As a barrio child in a Spanish-speaking home, I had difficulties relating to the Mary that I learned about in Catholic school. She seemed to be a person who never had to struggle. After all, she lived with Jesus, who was the Son of God, and Joseph, a saint! Her parents loved her, and they were saints, too. Mary had everything: what more could anybody ask for? What did she have to do with *me?*

But, as I came to understand, the virgin's name was not only Mary; it was also María, María of the Barrio— "Our Mary"—a *real* girl whom I and my friends could relate to because she was like us. "Our Mary" had skin color. (I remember looking at the "flesh" crayon in my Crayola box that didn't at all resemble my skin even in the winter when I "lost" my tan. What was "flesh-like" about that pale hue?) "Our Mary" had color, and she loved colorful things: flowing blue robes and mantillas made of real lace. Jewelry, too!

"Our Mary" shared our fiesta personalities. She loved parties—remember the wedding feast at Cana? As Latinos, we invited Mary to our fiestas and paraded her unabashedly around town, celebrating her presence and her closeness to us. Although God sometimes seemed too far away for most of us in the misery of the barrios, *María* was accessible. We trusted her and we loved her. We gave her affectionate nicknames and proudly called our children by them: Altagracia, Lupita, Caridad, Rosario, Esperanza, Dolores, Refugio. We named our *colmados* (grocery stores) and even our bars after her! She was part of daily life; she was one of us.

There isn't a Spanish-speaking country in the world that doesn't have a special version of Mary that is all their own. And each of us—*dominicanos, mexicanos, puertoriqueños, cubanos, nicaragüenses, salvadoreños,* etc.—has a special relationship with her because she has appeared to us, spoken to us in our native language, dressed like us, and looked like us. We feel protected and cherished because in our matriarchal culture, she is our *madrecita,* our dear mother. And this deep attachment can't be easily explained. As one devotee exclaimed, "I may be an atheist, but nobody touches my *Virgencita de Guadalupe!*" Let's face it: María is part of the Latino DNA no matter where we may roam.

Growing up with such a strong Marian culture deep in my bones, I couldn't help but feel that I needed to be like Mary. For a young person in the wild sixties, this was a challenge. Yet like Mary, I had choices, and with her help, I wanted to be faithful, as she had been.

When I was twelve, my single mother scraped together enough money to send me to boarding school in French-speaking Canada to keep me from "getting into trouble." Thankfully, Sister Yvonne and the other French nuns' attitude toward chastity drastically differed from that of the prevailing culture. They taught us girls that sex was of God and the "highest form of prayer; God is there where two individuals give of themselves totally and vulnerably in marriage." The nuns didn't tell us that this would be easy, but that it was nevertheless right. And they encouraged us to pray to Mary, who lived her chastity completely through virginity and who would help us make the same choice …until we might decide to marry.

And so, as difficult as it was—and it *was* difficult— I saved myself for my wedding night *completely,* not because I was going to be punished if I didn't, but because God sent an angel named Gabriel to Mary. My response could be no less than hers.

For me, Mary's "yes" that day in Nazareth had raised the bar. I accepted the same challenge and internalized Mary's loving action in my everyday, ordinary life. I began to believe that this "Mary of action," the one named after Miriam the prophetess, had to have been feisty, at least on the inside. It took feistiness and character to bear a child whose origin would have been questionable to others. And considering the times in which Mary lived, it must have been frightening for her to carry through with that pregnancy. To have her baby almost certainly meant death for Mary. But Mary not only obeyed. She trusted.

When I was pregnant with my fourth child, one of the doctors from my physicians' office ordered an abortion because I had contracted measles during the first trimester of my pregnancy.

"I refuse. There's a real baby in here." I pointed to the obvious place.

"The only solution in this case is an abortion." The obstetrician started to fill out the requisition.

"No! It's not an option."

"You are being very irresponsible." He threw the form at me.

"I will take my chances," I replied. "This is a *baby*. And I want him."

"Get out." He threw my file across his desk. I left, ripping up his abortion order and throwing it in the trash on my way out. Seven months later, it was a moment of triumph for me when the same doctor "just happened" to be assigned to deliver my baby. As it turned out, the "measles" was a rash from a new soap I had used; Carlos, my now brilliant and very handsome Ph.D. son, was born safe and sound.

On that day, I felt Mary's smile. She knew. *I* knew.

This feisty Mary continued to open my heart toward children: not only the children I bore, but the children of the world, too. I suppose the memory of Sister Yvonne's words helped me to hear this message more clearly. She always told us that "to whom much has been given much would be asked" (see Lk 12:48). She looked beyond the hurt and the poverty of the barrio girls in front of her and saw our dignity and our giftedness. She encouraged us to believe in ourselves. And although at first I couldn't believe on my own, I borrowed Sister Yvonne's belief until it became mine.

Gradually, I learned to accept my giftedness and to welcome the idea that "much would be asked" of me. I became an inner-city teacher and the mother of six incredible sons. And, with my feisty Mary still leading and guiding, I felt called to extend my motherhood to others, as she did at Jesus' request (see Jn 19:26–27). I began to take in children nobody else wanted—multiracial kids, older kids, learning-disabled kids, drug babies, sibling groups—and adopt them, first into my heart and then into my home. The first round of adoptions numbered six children. Years later, with the original twelve children all grown and doing well, I adopted a family of five children, ages two, four, five, eight, and thirteen. I was then fifty-nine, single, and very healthy.

Why did I accept such a vocation? There was a knock at the door of my heart one day. By the grace of God, I wasn't glazed over from TV watching, food, alcohol, or drugs. I wasn't on the back porch gossiping or too busy being busy. I was in a space where I could hear an invitation from God in just the way God chose to send it. So as crazy as it seemed to most people I knew, I opened the doors of my heart and home to these incredibly challenging and wonderful children.

Recently, I have heard yet another knock, another invitation to open my heart to God. Soon my young family and I will be going to spend three years as missionaries in the outskirts of Santa Cruz, one of the major cities of Bolivia, to help the street kids there.

Some people say I am crazy.

But how is it crazier than an impoverished teenage girl—a member of an oppressed people living in an occupied land—taking the chance of being stoned to death by her own people for her "unwanted" pregnancy, making her way uncomfortably on a donkey through desert, mountains, and streams, so close to giving birth...then watching her beautiful child and wondering what would become of him?

What could be crazier than that fiat she proclaimed for the sake of all God's people as a young girl so many years ago: "... *let it be with me according to your word*" (Lk 1:38)? We who love her and her Son can do no less. I truly believe Mary would serve the poor if she lived in our times.

Listen closely: there's a knocking at your door. An angel is there. He knows your name, and he has great news for you. Will you accept, as Mary did?

To Ponder

- What does your name mean? What calling might it imply for you?

- Growing up, what role did Mary play in your life?

- How do you regard the virtue of chastity in your life?

- What does Mary mean to you as you take the "next best step" on your spiritual journey?

- Are you ready for what God may ask of you?

Chapter 2

Mary's Journey of Faith

SELENA LIU, M. DIV., is a writer and social worker from Canada who lives in Los Angeles and works with children at risk in many parts of the world. She is a support group leader for children going through various stages of adoption and a trainer and educator for foster and adoptive parents. She has a B.A. in film and sociology and an M. Div. with a focus in counseling from Tyndale Seminary in Toronto.

In the sixth month the angel Gabriel was sent by God to a town in Galilee called Nazareth, to a virgin engaged to a man whose name was Joseph.... And he came to her and said, "Greetings, favored one! The Lord is with you!" But she was much perplexed by his words and pondered what sort of greeting this might be.

LUKE 1:26

WHEN I WAS A YOUNG CHILD, I used to look with envy at children who were being carried on their fathers' shoulders. It seemed so fun and free up there, seeing all there was to see. I'd watch them slip and slide and wave their arms, smiling and laughing. I imagined if only I could be high up like that, I'd feel free, exhilarated, and invincible, too. But while my dad has always been affectionate, carrying a child on his shoulders was just not one of the moves in his repertoire. So one day, when a friend of the family—but a stranger to me—asked if I wanted a ride on his shoulders, I enthusiastically accepted, thinking I'd feel on top of the world. But once up in the air, I immediately began screaming, kicking, and crying in fear. Being young, I didn't understand that the free feeling had much more to do with trust in the one carrying me than with the simple act of being high in the air. I didn't realize that in order to feel wonderful when out of control, you have to trust the one who *is* in control. As an adult, I now see a child relaxed and freely enjoying herself atop her father's shoulders as an intimate, trusting moment, a moment when, because of her trust in one whom she loves, the child can see so much more than her own, small world.

At the moment of the Annunciation, Mary was such a child, a girl hoisted by the Angel Gabriel onto the shoulders of her Father. He raised her up from her "child's perspective" of life and the world so that she could share the Father's view. Through Gabriel, it was as if God's invitation rang clear: "Mary, you of this little town of Nazareth, I want you to know that I love you. And I have something to show you." This is the language of intimacy. At that moment—perplexing because the teenaged Mary never expected such an invitation from her Father—she trusts that the voice is true. If she was calm and open, it was because the voice, though never heard audibly in the past, bore a message she recognized in faith.

Whether or not we are alert enough to recognize them, we all receive messages from God—and they follow a pattern similar to the pattern of God's annuncia-

tion to Mary, even if we don't hear a voice like Gabriel's
from the world beyond. An affirmation of relationship
happens first, and then a sense of being lifted up, called
to share God's vantage point, and invited to a divine
purpose. And the beauty of this "annunciation pattern"
lies in its mutuality: God chooses to act through us,
always in collaboration with our human openness.
Mary trusted in God, but God also trusted in Mary.

It is both perplexing and amazing that the God of
the universe would see us and choose to speak to us, as
he did to Mary. Believing this requires truckloads of
trust. I often ask myself: Do I trust that God wants
more for me than I could even want for myself? I'm so
ordinary! At times like these, a humorous story told by
a pastor from India always comes to mind. A tourist
visiting a rural Indian town asked the tour guide,
"Have there been any great men or women born in this
city?" The tour guide's answer was short and succinct:
"No, only babies." We all start from the same ordinary
humanness—the ordinariness that we share with Mary
of Nazareth.

There are "annunciation moments" in everyone's
life that are like divine "place-markers," whether they
appear to us as small incidents that remind us of God's
presence or defining moments of choice that serve as
radical markers on our journey. For Mary, the Annunciation was certainly a defining moment...but how hard
it must have been for Mary to tell her friends and fam-

ily that the Angel Gabriel appeared to her with the
news that she would be pregnant as a virgin! It can be
so tempting to explain away things that truly matter.
We don't want to invite others to criticize our sense of
normalcy by suggesting that we have had an inspiration—let alone a vision!—from God. Yet sometimes
God specifically chooses circumstances that challenge
our need to explain away his purpose. Perhaps this is
to help remind us of our humanity and our need to
trust in him. One of my own annunciation moments
occurred in a momentary flash when I was a young
child, returned to my life when I was a teenager, and
colored the rest of my life.

I was only seven years old, and Bobby was one of my
second grade classmates. It was winter, and we were
bundled up so thick we waddled. Near the end of a
lunch hour that we had spent laughing and sliding
down a snowy hill, Bobby decided he needed to tell me
something. To this day I remember exactly how he
looked in his puffy green jacket, the frosty air forming
clouds as he spoke. Bobby told me his father beat him
and that when he got really angry, he'd put rings on his
knuckles and start punching. Bobby pushed up his jacket and showed me his black-and-blue arm. I was scared,
but it sounded like a secret I wasn't supposed to share.
Then the bell rang, we turned to go inside, and that was
the end of our conversation. Soon after that, Bobby
moved out of the area and I never saw him again.

Seven years later, when I was fourteen, I had a recurring dream five nights in a row. Bobby was in each dream. I remember thinking, "Why am I dreaming about a boy I knew half my life ago?" I don't recall what the dreams were about, only that he was in them, and I didn't understand what they meant. But a week later, when a friend of mine called and said, "I heard that some kid who used to go to your old elementary school killed himself," I immediately answered, "I know. It was Bobby." At the funeral, I could not stop crying as I saw his casket carried down the aisle of the church, even though I hadn't seen him in so many years. No one ever knew the reasons for his suicide, but I could not help thinking about the secret we had shared as seven-year-olds so many years before. At that moment, without my realizing it, Bobby became my Gabriel, and his secret, my annunciation moment.

Today, I am a children's social worker; I spend my days with abused and neglected children. Sometimes I am tempted to tell others I have no idea how I got here, but I know there seems to be a greater will for my life than I have on my own, even if it's unclear at first. Just as Mary didn't know everything that her "yes" would mean, I didn't immediately realize the "career impact" of my relationship with Bobby or my dreams about him. I didn't realize that the events of the past would lead me to become a social worker, and there are days when I need to call to mind the annunciation moments that tell me God wants me here more than I desire it for myself. As much as we all desire to know our life's purpose with crystal clarity, most times God does not speak in clear, dramatic ways. But every once in a while, the clarity of vision and voice *does* come—and this clarity seems directly proportional to our need to muscle through the hardships a particular task requires. I have sometimes needed Bobby, maybe as much as Mary needed Gabriel. Her vision of the angel, as much as my remembrance of Bobby, probably sustained her for the hardships that were to come.

Mary's annunciation vision is what provided her with the strength to endure the long journey to Bethlehem, giving birth in a strange place, and having to flee unexpectedly to Egypt. And as we see in *The Nativity Story,* the challenges began long before those journeys: anyone in Nazareth who didn't believe her vision could have stoned Mary to death. Yet she met this possibility with courage. There are redemptive moments in life that don't seem to make sense from our vantage point, but from God's view they make perfect sense. Mary certainly had her share of times like these, and I can imagine her not as a child enjoying the freedom up on her Father's shoulders, but rather as one gripping him tightly, trusting him not to let her go.

Yet alongside the things that don't make sense, there is a lightness of being that comes from believing you are fulfilling your life's purpose; perhaps it was this knowledge that gave Mary her sense of humility blended with calm invincibility that in any other context would seem incompatible. In *The Nativity Story,* Mary assures both herself and Joseph by saying, "There is a will for this child greater than my fear of what they may do." Mary recognized that neither she nor Joseph were in control. We value control so much, and yet the times I have felt most secure have been times when God gave me a sense of assurance...and then seemed to take the task out of my hands. The difficult work I do, dependent on things so often beyond my control, is lightened by that sense of calling.

The children I work with are usually unable to feel the safety of being on the shoulders of their fathers. Many children I visit don't know what it is like to have a father at all, let alone one who would hold them and guide them. Every day, instead of faces that reflect the freedom and exhilaration that every child should feel in the arms of their parents, I see eyes that are filled with fear, deeply saddened by years of pain and abuse or, in the worst cases, deadened by neglect and disassociation from the world. But I have also seen moments of joy and hope when emotionally orphaned children snuggle up into the arms of their new parents and frozen faces melt into joy. I have seen parents who were deadened by their own pain wake up and get their lives together in order to earn their children's trust again. And I have seen Mary's calm and trust reflected in the response of adoptive parents, too, when the adoption process was in peril. When parents endure excruciatingly difficult times and can rise from these ashes, there is the strength that comes from believing, "Everything in my life has prepared me for this." With this kind of strength, extraordinary miracles can happen.

I have had one of those extraordinary miracles occur in my own life. As a social worker, I was scheduled to attend an appreciation breakfast honoring foster and adoptive parents, but nothing seemed to be going right as the day approached. It had already been a bad week financially, and I remember saying under my breath, "What next? Is my car going to break down?" Sure enough, speeding down the highway to the breakfast, I felt the power begin to drain from my vehicle until it stopped and refused to restart.

A series of strange "coincidences" involving several people who made great efforts to help me piqued my curiosity at the divine purpose that might be awaiting me. My annoyance over all the inconveniences gave way to a perplexed anticipation. The series of events were so strange, in fact, that the tow truck driver asked me, "Is there somewhere you *need* to be today?" I could only chuckle and respond, "I guess so!"

I was still smiling to myself as I pulled into the parking lot, forty-five minutes late for the event, not ever anticipating the seriousness to come. With the breakfast well underway, the lot was still and quiet. But as I got out of the car, I heard a familiar sound. There on a man's shoulders, screaming, kicking, and crying, a little boy was fighting for all he was worth. It was Jake, a three-year-old foster child I had been working with, a child who in his young life had already known at least five mothers and fathers. The man had the child's legs in an angry death grip and Jake—recognizing me lunged down for help. When I asked the man to identify himself, he claimed he was a foster parent taking the child for a walk to calm him down.

In fact, the man was attempting to kidnap Jake and my arrival on the scene thwarted his plan. If I had not been delayed and arrived late, Jake would have disappeared, perhaps forever. On that day, many people heard the voice of God, and God enabled each one to make sure I would be in the right place at the right time. Before then, Jake had been described as "a miracle waiting to happen." Three years later, the miraculous has again occurred; Jake is adopted, and there is no greater vision than seeing him snuggle into his mother and father's arms, completely trusting and free.

I often imagine that my feeling at peace about God's divine purpose in my life depends on how I envision my relationship with him. Do I envision God as a stranger leading me unyielding and struggling into the darkness of pain, danger, and loneliness? Or do I know him as a loving Father inviting me to put my small hands in his as he hoists me onto his shoulders, carrying me on an amazing journey beyond my imagination? Mary of Nazareth decided on the latter and was gifted with an incredible journey of eternal significance. In some small way, may each one of our journeys of faith follow hers.

To Ponder

- How does the Gospel account of the Annunciation speak to you (see Lk 1:26–38)? If you were a filmmaker, how would you imagine it to have happened?

- Reflect on the role of faith in your life and on your efforts to develop it.

- How does God ask you to live your faith in the community?

- How does Mary's faith influence your spiritual journey?

CHAPTER 3

Mary's Journey of Surrender

Marie Paul Curley, FSP, is a Daughter of St. Paul, a video producer, and an aspiring screenwriter. She is the author of *Life for the World: A Way of Eucharistic Adoration for Today,* coauthor of *Bread of Life: Prayers for Eucharistic Adoration,* and the editor of *Christ Lives in Me: The Eucharistic Spirituality of Blessed James Alberione.* She has a B.A. in Communications from Emmanuel College in Boston.

ary said to the angel, "How can this be, since I am a virgin?" The angel said to her, "The Holy Spirit will come upon you, and the power of the Most High will overshadow you; therefore the child to be born will be holy...." Then Mary said, "Here am I, the servant of the Lord; let it be with me according to your word."

LUKE 1:34, 35, 38

OF ALL THE EVENTS IN THE LIFE of Mary, the Mother of Jesus, the moment of the Annunciation seems to me to be her most vulnerable. In just an instant, this young teenage girl receives momentous news and surrenders her entire being to God. The Church is so in awe of the depth and fullness of Mary's "yes" that we are encouraged to pray thrice-daily the Angelus, in which we repeat Mary's profound words of surrender.

Surrender—a challenging word today. Our "do-it-yourself" Western culture shudders at the passivity such a word implies. Surrender doesn't sound like strength, but weakness. Submission. Giving up. Even...

defeat. As women called to be life-givers and nurturers, to stand up for the dignity of each person in a depersonalized society, how are we called to live a concept so counter-cultural? How do strength, faith, and maturity resonate with surrender? When we talk about Mary's journey of surrender, aren't we contradicting the idea of Mary as a strong woman of faith? Surrender seems like a betrayal of our hard-won self-determination and even threatens our image of ourselves.

As a woman of the twenty-first century, I am particularly sensitive to words that carry connotations of oppression, passivity, victimization, or mindless obedience, and I have found myself avoiding the whole idea of surrender. In fact, even my personality—proactive, intense, and anxious—makes just the *possibility* of surrender a struggle.

As a writer, I have repeatedly felt invited to surrender—and yet felt that surrender was impossible. Writing is a desire I've held from childhood that I have only recently rediscovered. It has now become part of who I am, a gift that enriches every part of my life. But at first, although I increasingly valued the time and ability to write I was being given, I also became increasingly anxious about anything to do with it; I asked myself: What will people think of my work? Is my writing process too slow? Am I writing honestly and deeply enough? The list could go on. At one point, my anxiety so paralyzed me that one paragraph could take hours to write. Living in such a heightened state of anxiety was too painful; I started to think about giving up writing entirely. Concerned friends repeatedly offered me the simple advice that I was trying too hard and simply needed to "let it go." In theory, I saw the value of letting go, but in real life I was too anxious to loosen my grip. Because creativity isn't something I can control, I guess I felt that I needed to maintain control on everything else.

Recently, however, I received an unexpected insight: the "letting go" my friends encouraged wasn't really enough. There is a huge difference between "letting go" and "surrendering." Letting go means abandoning my writing to free fall without a safety net. Surrendering, instead, means entrusting my writing to Another. Suddenly, surrender not only made sense, but became an important part of growing in my relationship with God.

In its essence, surrender to God is not about passivity at all; it is about trust. It is not something anyone can do *to you*; instead, it is one of the purest actions a believer can take, and it is always assisted by grace. Surrender cannot happen outside a relationship. Learning how to trust can be difficult; we have so often been betrayed by people in this world stained by original sin. God, however, is always trustworthy.

Trust must be the key to understanding Mary's surrender, and perhaps with this key, people like me who struggle with the idea of spiritual surrender can begin to unlock the mystery of this young woman's heart. For indeed, she had a heart that she threw open so wide to grace that through her the Savior entered our world.

Mary's call and surrender happened within the context of an encounter with God. In the Scriptures, an angel is a manifestation of God. I wonder what it is really like to see an angel. Perhaps seeing Gabriel was enough for Mary to experience in a new way God's tremendous love for her. And Gabriel's first words, "Rejoice, Mary!"—which troubled her—revealed unexpectedly how beloved she was in God's eyes.

As a devout Jewish girl, Mary's relationship with God would have been honest, tender, and *real*. Mary's words in the Gospels disclose not only her immense faith and spirit of prayer, but also her "at-homeness," or comfort, with the Scriptures. The ranting of the psalms, the exultant yet tender promises of Isaiah—she must have pondered and prayed with all these emotions and heard her parents and neighbors do so as well. Gabriel's appearance must have confirmed for Mary, in some mysterious way we can only imagine, the vast reality of God's love that she had often pondered and prayed in the Scriptures.

The call of God always happens within relationship. Moses asked God to tell him the name of God. Paul on the road to Damascus asked Jesus, "Who are you?" Abram and Sarai received new names. Being chosen means, first of all, discovering one's identity as the beloved of God. I remember when I first realized God might be calling me to religious life. I was a teenager. And my overwhelming response (after shock) was huge, uncontainable joy. For the first time in my life, I *felt*—almost as a physical certainty—God's incredibly deep love for me. Despite how nervous I was about leaving my family, the radiance of God's love and my confidence that God would be faithful no matter what dimmed any concerns. Continually, people who knew me would stop and ask, "What's happened? Why are you *glowing*?" I couldn't explain it, but the joy of being beloved overflowed even into my physical appearance.

This certainty that she is beloved of God must have given Mary the courage to ask, after the stupendous news of the angel, one simple question: "How can I become the Mother of God's Son if I am a virgin?" Mary was aware that an unmarried pregnant woman would suffer disgrace, be considered an outcast, and even be condemned to death by stoning, as we see clearly in the film *The Nativity Story*. A mysterious pregnancy would forever change Mary's relationship with Joseph. In allowing that relationship to be placed in jeopardy, Mary gives up all security for the future. With her one question, Mary shows her awareness that by responding with a "yes" to God's call, she is literally putting her future—and her very life—in God's hands.

And this is just what Mary does. Her incredible response reveals like nothing else the depth of her trust and the exclusivity of her commitment to God. "Here am I, the servant of the Lord; let it be with me according to your word" (Lk 1:38).

The fullness of Mary's assent to God's invitation points to an unspoken aspect of surrender that Mary lived: virginity consecrated to God. A woman religious who consecrates her virginity to God as Mary did surrenders to the Lord absolutely everything she is: body, soul, future potential, and the fruit of her body: children. Consecrated virginity leads to a particular kind of intimacy with God. When a wife enters into the marriage covenant with her husband, she is constantly learning to know him in the most intimate ways possible: his every mood, his deepest dreams, the contours of his body and his soul. Likewise, a consecrated religious woman enters into a covenant relationship with God: Father, Son, and Spirit. She learns to recognize the radiance of God's smile, God's dance of joy in creation, the sadness of God in the eyes of suffering children and the marginalized people in the world, and the "still small voice," that whisper of God's inspiration. While consecrated virginity as a vocation is more the exception than the rule, it is a model of the depth of trust in God that every Christian is called to live, a trust that Mary lived throughout her entire life and that shines through even the words of her "yes" to God.

Pondering her words might give us further insight into that depth of trust. Besides the Magnificat, Mary's recorded words are sparse. Her response to Gabriel seems unexpectedly lengthy: "Here am I, the servant of the Lord; let it be with me according to your word" (Lk 1:38). She could have easily said it all in one word: "Yes." Or she could have cut her response in half: "Here I am, Lord"—a classic response to the call of God in the Hebrew Scriptures. But if we look attentively, we see that Mary's response is not one word too long: the combination of the two sentences reveals the depth of her relationship with God.

"Here I am" is a statement that is open-ended and ready; with it, Mary gives herself over completely. Combined with the following words, "the servant of the Lord," this simple assertion reveals the incredible totality of Mary's availability. As we saw earlier, *nothing* is off-limits to God in Mary's life; because of her relationship with her God, she gives herself completely to God and God's work.

Putting these two phrases together makes them proactive—"in your face," in the language of popular culture. Mary not only declares her readiness; she also defines it in terms of servitude. To serve is to be in active collaboration *with*. This is the response of a practical woman who knows that raising a child requires giving her life and her heart; this is the response of a woman who knows (along with Joseph) that raising the Son of

God will require unique sacrifices, leaps of faith in the dark, and a heart broken again and again by her Son's sufferings. Mary understands that she is being asked to do something that will take everything she has and is— and she *still* says "yes."

Mary's second sentence perfectly completes the first: "Let it be with me according to your word" (Lk 1:38). If in the first sentence she actively commits to this call of God, in this second sentence she entrusts all the results back to God. Even the structure of her sentence (as it is translated into English) is in the passive voice, a complete entrusting of the action to one outside herself. These are the words of a woman who is clear about what is and isn't hers to do; these are the words of a woman who understands that God's work truly is God's. Mary entrusts to God what is not her responsibility: the response of Joseph and the village; people's response to her Son; the direction her life will take; all the unknowns she is agreeing to in this moment. Mary recognizes that she cannot control outcomes. She gives fully what she has and surrenders everything else into God's hands: "Let it be...."

Mary's words are the perfectly balanced response to all my own misgivings about surrender: my fear of letting go of control, of giving up my own desires and way of doing things, of dying to myself in a culture that celebrates self-indulgence. Mary's response shows me the

ideal balance between actively giving myself completely to God with all the strength, love, joy, and intelli-
gence God has given me, and surrendering all that I
would like to control but am unable to: the well-being
of my loved ones, what others think of what I write,
and the results of my efforts in the mission of my religious community.

In the past I tried to control my relationship with
God. Now, rather than asking God to show his love for
me, I ask for the grace to recognize the ways he is loving me in my life...on a daily basis. No longer do I need
to make demands on God; rather, I ask God to let me
experience his presence and action in my life, in my situation.

Lately, God seems to be inviting me to surrender
even those things *inside of me* over which I am power-
less: my inadequacies, my tendency to doubt God, my
anxious personality. Every surrender is a "little death,"
but each time I discover that, I emerge lighter, happier,
and freer to focus on God's invitation in the moment.

The Annunciation was not Mary's ultimate surrender, but the *beginning* of her life's journey that led to the
ultimate surrender of her Son at Calvary. Her life gives
hope to us, whose acts of surrender may be very personal and sometimes dramatic, but perhaps not as complete. Surrendering to God is an ongoing journey. The
surrender of our life, our health, someone we love, or

something we love to do is an ongoing dance with our Loving Partner in which we must trust how God will lead us at each step, even if it is into the unknown.

The pain inherent in every act of surrender doesn't need to blind us to its fruit: the joy of responding to God's unique love for us by removing any limits to that love that we may have set up along the way. Each time we surrender to God, we make a new act of surrender possible; in this way, surrender becomes a virtue, a habit of being. Mary radiated the joy of her surrender to God in her Magnificat, the canticle of praise she prays when she journeys to visit Elizabeth shortly after the Annunciation. Each of us is called by God to live in that same joy and freedom, from "Here am I, the servant of the Lord; let it be with me according to your word" (Lk 1:38), to "My soul magnifies the Lord, and my spirit rejoices in God my Savior" (Lk 1:47).

To Ponder

- What is the difference between passivity and action? Between resignation and surrender?

- Have you ever prayed with Mary, "Here I am, Lord, let it be done unto me according to your word"? Did something change because of your prayer?

- How well do you know yourself? How would
  you characterize yourself before the Lord? What
  do you need, and what do you want?

- Do you believe that God loves you? What is your
  image of God, and how does this influence your
  prayer and your spiritual journey?

CHAPTER 4

Mary's Journey to Elizabeth

JUDITH ANN ZIELINSKI, OSF, is a Sylvania (Ohio) Franciscan who has worked in Church communications for over twenty-five years. She has written and produced numerous award-winning domestic and international TV programs. Her latest documentary, *Jesus Decoded,* produced in 2006 for the U.S. Catholic bishops, aired on NBC stations across the country.

" And now, your relative Elizabeth in her old age has also conceived a son; and this is the sixth month for her who was said to be barren. For nothing is impossible with God...." In those days Mary set out and went with haste to a Judean town in the hill country, where she entered the house of Zechariah and greeted Elizabeth.

LUKE 1:36, 39–40

WHEN I REFLECT ON THE STORY of Mary traveling to visit her cousin Elizabeth, what first staggers me—literally and symbolically—is the hill.

The Gospel of Luke says that, following the Annunciation, *"Mary set out and went with haste to a Judean town in the hill country, where she entered the house of Zechariah and greeted Elizabeth"* (Lk 1:39). Although Luke does not mention the name of the town, some scholars—and early Christian writers—believe the probable site to be the village of Ain Karem, located approximately midway between Jerusalem and Bethlehem—an easy walking distance for the young Mary.

Still—that hill! On my first trip to Israel, our tour bus driver took one look at it, politely cut the bus engine, and hissed open the door. We were out on our feet, like Mary in the "hill country" to visit Elizabeth.

In 1997, I went to Israel as a member of a parish pilgrimage—about forty-five of us from Santa Monica, California. Our itinerary included all the Christian and Marian sites and shrines mentioned in the New Testament. Ain Karem—the traditional site of Mary's visit with Elizabeth and proclamation of the Magnificat—would be my favorite, a place that began the slow turning of my heart toward Mary.

Despite my childhood's Catholic upbringing—full of Marian hymns, May processions, membership in the "Children of Mary" sodality, the recitation of countless family rosaries, and the consistent encouragement of the sisters who taught me—I had always had an uneasy relationship with Mary. Even after professing vows as a Franciscan religious, Marian devotion remained marginal for me. Why pray to Mary when Jesus was available—loving, forgiving, and accessible? The usual rationale I had been taught—that Mary used a Mother's power of intercession with her Son for us and that her role as "one of us" helped her to understand our common human challenges—never spoke deeply to me, and as I grew up, my Marian devotion never blossomed.

Now in the Holy Land as a pilgrim, I looked forward to experiencing all of the holy places, but as a television professional, I was also interested in the sites associated with Mary. I wondered if there was a television documentary lurking anywhere. Besides all of that, I also wondered if being in and walking through the Holy Land, seeing the Marian sites firsthand, would help me discover a Mary I had yet to meet and with whom I could bond.

Once up that steep hill in Ain Karem, panting from middle-aged fatigue, I passed through the lovely wrought-iron gate at its top and immediately sensed a "femininity" at the site. The mood was gentle, peaceful, simple. Unlike Nazareth, with its immense basilica over the cave of the Annunciation, and the dark underground crypt of the nativity in Bethlehem, this spot felt fresh, intimate, and open, with its curving stone arches covered with flowers and vines.

I looked up at the façade of the Church of the Visitation and its mosaic commemorating Mary's visit to her older cousin Elizabeth. Luke writes that Mary "entered the house of Zechariah and greeted Elizabeth" (Lk 1:41). As with most Holy Land shrines, no original or "official" house existed where this greeting took place. Instead, a church was built over the site to commemorate that Scripture event that has drawn pilgrims for centuries. Luke continues:

> When Elizabeth heard Mary's greeting, the child leaped in her womb. And Elizabeth was filled with the Holy Spirit and she exclaimed with a loud cry,

"Blessed are you among women, and blessed is the fruit of your womb. And why has this happened to me that the mother of my Lord comes to me? For as soon as I heard the sound of your greeting, the child in my womb leaped for joy" (Lk 1:41–44).

Here was the older woman, who had been childless, barren, and seemingly forgotten by God, embracing and celebrating her young cousin. Mary and Elizabeth, separated by age but united by the hand of God, fell into each others' arms. Young Mary must have been bursting with bewilderment, wonder, amazement, and anxiety after her encounter with Gabriel: *Why? How? When?* Mary was probably still dazed by the angel's message, anxious about the coming questions and whispers she would face from her family and neighbors in Nazareth, unsure of how to handle her pregnancy, and uncertain of what to say to Joseph. Little wonder she fled to see this older woman whom she trusted!

As we gathered inside the courtyard, our Christian tour guide explained that in tribal societies unmarried pregnant women were often stoned—and by their own male relatives. This practice continues today in rural areas where the culture can be fiercely judgmental of women who step outside the conservative, harsh social norms. The guide explained that Mary's "yes" to Gabriel acknowledged the very real possibility of this outcome. Mary knew that her own life could be in jeopardy, that she could be stoned as a "loose woman," a sinner, a harlot. But her "yes" allowed God to intervene in the lives of her people, and that "yes"—spoken for the good of the community—overrode her fears for her personal safety and reputation. Indeed, no wonder Mary ran to Elizabeth! She needed to talk, to cry, to ask, to listen, to share what was in her heart. This was a Mary far removed from the placid blue-and-white-robed figure I had grown up with. This was a woman of courage: a flesh-and-blood woman who, with hammering heart, made her noble choice for the greater good. She said "yes" not out of fear but out of generosity and freedom—and paid an emotional price for doing so.

Elizabeth, pregnant beyond *her* childbearing years, was probably also the talk of neighbors and friends; long barren yet surprisingly fertile, she must have felt unsure of the mystery in her own womb. Her husband, mute because of his own doubt about their ability to conceive, waited with her in silence. It was no longer life or marriage "as usual." They were two elderly people, husband and wife, who had always lived their lives in fidelity to God, and then, crazily, when they should have been spending their years peacefully waiting for death, they faced an extraordinary journey. Their son would, "With the spirit and the power of Elijah...prepare for the Lord a people fit for him" (Lk 1:17). What mysteries did they contemplate together as Elizabeth's belly swelled with her pregnancy?

Mary and Elizabeth clasped each other as only they could. Age and youth, virgin and matron, they were two unsuspecting women whom God had plucked from their lives of sheer ordinariness to bring about the mystery of human salvation. No wonder Elizabeth exclaimed, "And blessed is she who believed that there would be a fulfillment of what was spoken to her by the Lord" (Lk 1:45). The Lord had spoken to both of them, and both were blessed in their belief.

The humanity, the *absolutely-yes-I-would-have-done-the-same-thing* femininity of their encounter touched me deeply. I felt a connection to these two women who, because of the unbelievable forces that had just exploded in their lives, sought each other out to confide, to encounter wisdom, to reflect on and understand God's action. How often are we moved to do the same with trusted friends?

Then Mary proclaimed one of the greatest prayer-poems in the Scriptures: the Magnificat. Many Scripture scholars say that this poem was probably not uttered from Mary's lips as a whole. The verses hearken back to another Old Testament canticle, and it may be a compilation of verses added on later. Whatever the Magnificat's origins, it has come down to us as Mary's signature statement—her remarkable proclamation of faith, awareness, strength, humility, and even politics. I imagine Mary really did utter it in Elizabeth's presence:

"My soul magnifies the Lord,
and my spirit rejoices in God my Savior,
for he has looked with favor on the lowliness of his
    servant.
Surely, from now on all generations will call me
    blessed;
for the Mighty One has done great things for me, and
    holy is his name" (Lk 1:46–49).

Mary begins with an expression of humility: she knows who she is and who she is before God. God has lifted her up: without him, she would be nameless and unremembered. On my personal "re-meeting-Mary-meter," I noted her self-awareness and sense of practicality. She was very much in touch with reality and could articulate her before-and-after relationship with God and the world. She knew that this encounter changed everything. I liked the fact that she "got it."

Her prayer continues:

"His mercy is for those who fear him
from generation after generation.
He has shown strength with his arm;
he has scattered the proud in the thoughts of their
    hearts.
He has brought down the powerful from their
    thrones,
and has lifted up the lowly;
he has filled the hungry with good things,
and sent the rich away empty" (Lk 1:50–55).

Here Mary speaks as a woman of her tribe. She is a voice for her people, oppressed and living in an occupied land. The Romans controlled their access to travel, taxed them, set up harsh rulers over them, ridiculed their faith, and limited their freedom in countless ways. The Romans' rule was complete and ruthless. For every Jew who attempted a revolt, participated in an organized protest, or stepped out of line, the Romans answered with a torturous death—often crucifixion. Mary and her people lived daily under the thumb of oppression. And yet in the Magnificat, she fearlessly and confidently proclaims her faith in God: he had brought down rulers from their thrones and had lifted up the lowly before— and he would do so again. The oppression of her people would not last forever; in God's good time, he would rescue them again. He would change the reality, turn the tables: he would "fill the hungry with good things and send the rich away empty." The Magnificat as a political statement? This was an interpretation I had never made before. What power these words held in Mary's time, uttered from her mouth! They signified a creed, a belief in what appeared impossible: the toppling of an overwhelming enemy. This Mary was not the "Holy Mary" of my childhood. She was a woman facing down the dictator, in solidarity with her community, standing alongside and for the oppressed, the poor, and the downtrodden. This Mary had quiet nerve—she was a "steel magnolia."

Over the next two weeks, as our bus rolled on from one point to another in the Holy Land, crossing into the "occupied territories" where Palestinian Arabs (Christians and Muslims) lived, Mary's Magnificat rang in my ears. Nothing has really changed in two thousand years. Still oppressed, many of the people live in ghettos and behind barbed-wire fences. They are forced to stop at checkpoints, subjected to searches, denied access to hospitals and jobs. A generation of people is growing up without education, living in hovels, without running water, electricity, civic services, police protection, banks, or social infrastructure. After years of resistance and *intifadah,* the people suffer despair, manipulated by terrorist factions and inept leadership and brainwashed by political operatives. Many willingly sacrifice their very bodies as weapons in the desperate struggle. I saw these villages and the poverty of these people, and I heard Mary's words again.

The Magnificat was no longer simply a 2,000-year-old scriptural prayer; it was a defiant cry against oppression everywhere, a proclamation that God's reign would one day lift up the poor and lowly, that justice would reign on this earth, and that the rich and the poor, the well-fed and the hungry, the voiceless and the powerful, would change places.

Outside the Church of the Visitation, I wandered into the Court of the Magnificat. Mounted on stone walls were plaques bearing the words of the Magnificat in fifty languages. I watched as pilgrims of every nationality searched for the plaque written in their own language, and, reading, their lips moved in recognition of Mary's words.

How true had become the words she had uttered: "This day, all generations will call me blessed." We remember Mary not because she accomplished something significant by human standards, but because she grasped the enormity of the idea offered her by God through Gabriel: *To collaborate with God for the sake of the people, to launch the coming of the Kingdom—to birth God!* She would contain within her finite womb the immensity of the divine, and in so doing, she would forego the safety of the familiar and launch into the deep. As strange as it sounds, the words that open every Star Trek TV episode apply to her: *"To boldly go where no one has gone before."* No one has ever done what Mary did; her role as Mother of God is unique.

Meeting Mary in the Holy Land changed my life. She was not, after all, a wimp, not someone meekly handing over our intercessions to Jesus as they rolled down a heavenly assembly line. She was a heroine, a warrior for justice and the forgotten children of earth, with a spirit large enough to put aside her own safety and comfort for the sake of her entire people—including us. She was a woman of heart and spirit and faith. She is great because she swallowed and took the chance to allow God to make her great.

A television documentary did eventually emerge from my trip—a one-hour program for public television aptly called *Mary of Nazareth: From Icon to Woman.* That show brought me back to the Holy Land to introduce Mary to audiences who might not have had the privilege of meeting her as I had. She had indeed moved from icon to woman for me; she had become the mother, friend, and confidante she had never before been in my life. The climb up that hill to Ain Karem was worth the effort to meet the Mary of the Magnificat. In Ain Karem I met a Mary I never knew.

To Ponder

- Who is Mary for you?

- In this contemporary, secular age, do you think it is possible for people to believe that nothing is impossible for God?

- Resolve to make a pilgrimage to your cathedral, a Marian shrine, or another holy place. Try to do so in silence, with the intention of listening to God's word in a new way.

- Write a canticle of praise to God for the good things in your life.

CHAPTER 5

Mary's Journey of the Spirit

GRETCHEN HAILER, RSHM, is a full-time consultant in faith formation who specializes in curriculum design, media literacy, and spirituality. She is a frequent presenter at major religious education conferences and retreats in the U.S.A. and abroad. With Sr. Rose Pacatte, FSP, she is the coauthor of *Media Mindfulness: Educating Teens about Media and Faith* (St. Mary's Press).

And Mary said,
"My soul magnifies the Lord,
and my spirit rejoices in God my Savior,
for he has looked with favor on the lowliness of his
  servant.
Surely, from now on all generations will call me
  blessed;
for the Mighty One has done great things for me,
and holy is his name.
His mercy is for those who fear him
from generation to generation.
He has shown strength with his arm;
he has scattered the proud in the thoughts of their
  hearts.
He has brought down the powerful from their
  thrones,
and lifted up the lowly;
he has filled the hungry with good things,
and sent the rich away empty.
He has helped his servant Israel,
in remembrance of his mercy,
according to the promise he made to our ancestors,
to Abraham and to his descendants forever."

LUKE 1:46–55

In the Scriptures "the journey" is one of the most familiar metaphors used to symbolize our search for God. We see it in the Hebrew Scriptures when the various prophets are called and then sent out to speak God's word to the Israelites. Often it is a word of comfort, more often a word of challenge. God not only asks the *prophets* to move to another place, but the people as well. The place to which God calls them may require a geographical shift, but more likely it is a call to a change of attitude, a change of perspective. This kind of change is called conversion, and it directs the inner journey of the person intent on finding God. The call to conversion lasts a lifetime; every day the believer chooses to listen to God and to change.

When we consider Mary's spiritual journey, we also consider a call and a sending forth. Her initial call through the angel-messenger Gabriel was first introduced by words of comfort, "the Lord is with you." But at the same time, Mary is frightened and challenged and so she asks, "How can this be?" In this encounter we notice how Mary is direct and honest, courageous and open to the incredible message that she has received. We notice that she doesn't run to her mother or father for permission, nor does she seek advice from friends; she answers with a confident "yes." This immediate response provides strong evidence of her already deep relationship with her God; a relationship that prepared her to be sent forth as God desired.

This annunciation scene underlines what Paul was to write years later in the Letter to the Galatians, "When the fullness of time had come, God sent his Son, born of a woman" (Gal 4:4). At the moment of Mary's "yes," everything changed! Through Mary, Jesus came into this world to show us—in a personal way—the depths of God's love. Her Son, Jesus, the prophet par excellence, proclaimed God's words of comfort and challenge. Through Mary, Jesus not only became God's Word as a human being, but also the very road map for our journey.

The Annunciation has always been a favorite feast of mine, partially because in medieval times it was considered the first day of the year. The appropriate greeting on that day was "Happy New Year" because Mary's "yes" had made all things new. As a teenager, I found Mary's response rather fascinating. She was only my age, and yet she knew her truth, her inner strength. I began relating to her, not as my mother, but as my older sister. And years later when I became involved in ecumenical dialogue, I found that my Episcopalian, Lutheran, and Protestant friends, especially the women, often referred to Mary as their sister, reaffirming my relationship with Mary.

As a Religious of the Sacred Heart of Mary and a longtime teacher, I recall that at the beginning of every written assignment, we invited our students to write at the top of the page: *All for Jesus through Mary!* The exclamation point was an important part of the practice because it expressed a personal, enthusiastic response to the offering. This simple practice highlighted part of our congregation's spirituality. Our founder, Jean Gailhac, said it clearly in a letter he wrote to the sisters in 1882: "When we study Jesus through Mary, in Mary, we will not lose sight of any of the characteristics of Jesus."

When we look at Mary in Scripture, we are able to trace important points in her spiritual journey and come to look at her unique spirituality from different angles. Spirituality is often easier to observe than to define. Essentially, it is the unique way each of us lives out our faith each day in relationship with God. We all have a spirituality—whether we've identified it or not, and even if we do not actively admit it exists. It is that way of life that arises from the very center of our being and provides both focus and energy to our everyday choices and activities. As Christians, we believe that all the baptized have a spirituality, a particular gift of the spirit for the good of the community. Mary, too, had a spirituality, her own unique way of following God's spirit in her life.

As Christians we have come to realize that Mary was, indeed, the first disciple. Since she "pondered these things in her heart" (Lk 2:19), she was a believer in the truest sense of the word. She listened to God in the depths of her being and allowed God to reveal to her, probably little by little, that her Son was destined for a special mission. And as he grew into that mission, she noticed what energized him, observing his characteristics through a mother's eyes. She reflected on her experiences with him at Nazareth and observed a pattern to his spirituality, noticing how he rose early in the morning and went apart to pray. Even from his twelfth year, when she and Joseph discovered him in the Temple, she knew of his relationship with the One he called Father. And later she saw how the energy he gained from that relationship shaped his ministry to those on the margins of society as well as those who held earthly power.

After her initial consternation regarding reports she received about his teaching (Mk 3:21), Mary realized that his words resonated within her as well. Perhaps some of the parables Jesus used in his preaching originated with Mary and Joseph telling stories around the table at meals or whispering them in his ears as he fell asleep. As a human person, Jesus depended, like all of us, on the care of his parents. Just as we remember stories we've heard from our family, so, too, must have Jesus. Of course his mother was a formative influence in his life. But in addition, she, like the other disciples, would have sat down at the feet of Jesus to hear the Good News of the Kingdom.

Often we think of Mary as a blue-eyed, blonde-haired, demure-looking young woman dressed in blue! We've been led to that image by the many statues that we've seen of her on church pedestals or by romantic paintings of her in chapels, museums, or reproduced in books. In reality, given the time in which she lived, Mary would certainly not have been the "shrinking violet" that so many artists have visualized! And she probably never wore blue in her life; because of its rarity as a dye, only wealthy women could afford that color. Mary's colors were probably earthy: beige and brown. She lived in an occupied, third-world country; was probably not well schooled; was married to a construction worker; and, because she was a woman, lived on the margins of the liturgical life of her religion and the political reality of her society as well.

So how would we characterize Mary's spirituality? Its chief characteristics seem to me to have been an immediacy in her relationship with God and a solidarity with those on the margins of things.

Like her Son, she "pondered things in her heart" (Lk 2:19). Several times in Luke's account of the Gospel (and in the film *The Nativity Story*), Mary treasures or ponders life's events. This sense of immediacy to God's realm uncovers a deep attachment to the things of God. I like to imagine her praying the ancient words of the psalms—Israel's prayer songs—during her long trip to visit her kinswoman Elizabeth. She may not have been able to read or write, but because she belonged to a culture that was highly aural, she would have known her Scripture by heart. Those psalm prayers address all the many ways that our prayer rises up to God: adoration, thanksgiving, petition, and sorrow. How appropriate it would have been, therefore, for Mary to have prayed them during her journey to Elizabeth.

The second characteristic I would recognize in Mary's spirituality is that of solidarity with people who live on the margins of society. This is indeed the very point of the wonderful canticle which Mary utters when she is with Elizabeth. After learning of her own pregnancy, Mary's first concern was to make a helpful visit to her aged, pregnant kinswoman many miles away, probably traveling on foot. But whether riding on a wagon or a donkey or walking, Mary "walked the talk" of her faith; she lived her spirituality, she journeyed with God.

It is in her Magnificat (Lk 1:46–55) that we see the powerful Mary, a compelling model for all believers. In that prayer—which shows her tremendous understanding of the holy writings of her people, an understanding probably gleaned from quiet moments of immediacy with her God—Mary shows us what it means to be a disciple. The Magnificat is the longest speech attributed to Mary in the Gospels. It is a song of joy and praise that illustrates her trust in God. Mary relies on God to right the wrongs of her society—and ours as well. In a world where greed, selfishness, and oppression enslave many, Mary preaches liberation from the effects of personal and social sin—a liberation that will pave the way for her Son's life and teaching to truly transform the world. In our times, characterized by globalization, when money talks and the weak are forced to serve the strong, the first disciple of Jesus gives a different message. Millions of people around the world remember Mary's vocation, her response and challenge, as they pray the Magnificat daily in the prayer of the Church, the Liturgy of the Hours.

In the film *The Nativity Story,* we get a sense of Mary's joy at becoming the Mother of God when she greets Elizabeth. But even more, we feel Mary's understanding of the far-reaching implications of what it will mean for her—and for us—to follow her Son, when she says that God has "cast down the mighty from their thrones, and lifted up the lowly."

As a catechist, I often lead a workshop called, "Will the Real Mary Please Stand Up?" I developed this workshop for two reasons. First, because of my own personal journey of coming to know Mary better through the charism of my religious community and that image of Mary in my teenage years as my older sister. The other reason I think this seminar is important is because believers understand Mary's role in our lives in as many different ways as we see her image depicted—from icons to the recent bright graffiti image of Our Lady of Guadalupe painted on a wall of my East Los Angeles neighborhood. The real Mary is scriptural: at once a daughter, wife, cousin, friend, mother, and teacher who is strong and tender. She communicates Jesus to us and draws people together to follow Jesus by living the Beatitudes.

Mary proclaims that each one of us is a child of God, well loved and full of dignity. She challenges us to servanthood and community by her example and in the words of the Magnificat. This is both Mary's spirituality *and* Marian spirituality.

To Ponder

- How would you characterize your own spiritual journey?

- To what extent do you possess a sense of immediacy to God in your everyday life? How do you pray?

- What do you make of Mary's words in the Magnificat? How do they seem to bring us to the margins of society to preach a word of comfort?

- In what way does hope play a part in Mary's Magnificat?

Chapter 6

Mary's Journey
of Love

MARILYN-ANN ELPHICK, M.Div., Th.D. (candidate), is a registered nurse with over thirty-three years of experience. She currently works full time at the University of St. Michael's College, Toronto, Canada, as director of chaplaincy services and campus minister and part time as a registered nurse in the Hemodialysis Unit at the Toronto General Hospital. She is currently pursuing a doctorate in pastoral theology at the Faculty of Theology at the University of St. Michael's College, and she and her husband live just outside of Toronto.

Now the birth of Jesus the Messiah took place in this way. When his mother Mary had been engaged to Joseph, but before they lived together, she was found to be with child from the Holy Spirit. Her husband Joseph, being a righteous man and unwilling to expose her to public disgrace, planned to dismiss her quietly. But just when he had resolved to do this, an angel of the Lord appeared to him in a dream and said, "Joseph, son of David, do not be afraid to take Mary as your wife, for the child conceived in her is from the Holy Spirit. She will bear a son, and you are to name him Jesus, for he will save his people from their sins." All this took place to fulfill what had been spoken by the Lord through the prophet: "Look, the virgin shall conceive and bear a son, and they shall name him Emmanuel," which means, "God is with us." When Joseph awoke from sleep, he did as the angel of the Lord commanded him; he took her as his wife, but had no marital relations with her until she had borne a son; and he named him Jesus.

MATTHEW 1:18–25

THIS IS A LOVE STORY, and like any love story, it is marked by moments of drama, confusion, joy, and pain. Unlike any other love story, this story of a woman and a man is marked by a unique and intimate participation in God's plan. The woman was young by our standards, but at age fourteen or fifteen, she was an appropriate age for marriage in her culture and time. The Gospels offer us few details about Mary's early life, but we can imagine, as does the film *The Nativity Story,* that at first, Mary (or Miriam in Hebrew) may not have been too happy when her father announced her betrothal to Joseph; she very well may have wanted a say in whom she would marry. In the film, Joaquim and Anna decided to arrange for her marriage because they were poor and they knew Joseph (Yousef), though older than Mary, was strong in a gentle kind of way. Like other girls her age, Mary would have wondered about the man she would marry, but she was in no hurry. She stood on the threshold between childhood and womanhood—anxious yet reticent to move into this new reality. As soon as her parents told her of her betrothal, she knew she would no longer be able to play with her friends when she finished her household chores. As she helped a young mother draw water from the village well for her jar, she could see just how different her life would soon be.

After her natural reaction to her father's decision, she must have felt shy when she thought of living with

Joseph, wondering if they would ever love one another. We can imagine that Anna assured her that these feelings would deepen when she was more mature. Mary could not have guessed that within twenty-four hours, a series of wondrous events would launch her into that unknown territory called womanhood.

∞

YESTERDAY, HER DREAMS were about her future, and today all things seemed to hang in a state of suspended animation. Had an angel actually appeared to her asking her to be the mother of the Anointed One? Mary replayed the scene in her head. Suddenly she became aware that she had paused only for an instant before she uttered "yes" because she loved God more than anything—more than even life itself. Yesterday. Was it only yesterday that she was a child working and playing with her friends in the village? Today, she was *with* child and realized that she must put aside her childish ways and thoughts. She had changed overnight and, although she could not fathom the extent of this change, she was a woman.

There was no time to ease into this new reality. There had been no time to think about the consequences until now. Mary began to shake uncontrollably as the full impact of last night's events broke through her consciousness. Her mind began to spew out doubts with volcanic force, threatening to suffocate her with a torrent of misgivings, qualms, and uncertainties. What would Joseph do? He had every right to cancel the marriage, and that would never be forgotten in the village. Her poor child would carry the scars. She felt the protective pangs of motherhood spring up in her breast and firmly take hold of her heart. Suddenly she hugged her stomach fiercely as if to say to her unborn child, "I love you so much already. No one will hurt you or harm you as long as I am alive."

She was with child before she and Joseph were to live together. Mary then did what many do when caught in an untenable position—she left in order to have time to sort things out. She informed her parents that she wanted to visit her cousin Elizabeth. Though surprised, her parents permitted her to go. They, and Joseph as well, were confused by her sudden decision.

Mary and Elizabeth were overjoyed to see one another because they knew how God had intervened in their lives. After spending some months with Elizabeth and Zechariah in the village of Ain Karem, just a few short miles from Jerusalem as tradition has it, Mary returned to Nazareth. She had seen the birth of John and witnessed Zechariah's newfound ability to speak. She had uttered the words of her Magnificat; her spirit truly rejoiced in God, her Savior.

Joseph, Joaquim—indeed everyone in Nazareth—was shocked when they noticed Mary's pregnancy.

Joseph was angry and confused. But Mary's desire to protect her child was stronger than her fear at what others would think of her. Perhaps in her heart she prayed again, "I am your handmaiden, Lord; give me the strength and courage to do your will." Later, when Mary tried to explain that she had conceived through the Holy Spirit, neither her parents nor Joseph believed her. Perhaps Joseph felt small, insignificant, and hopeless that Mary had made a fool of him as he watched the dreams of their life together become like grains of sand in a desert storm; there was nothing left to hold on to. Life would never be the same again. Joseph was plagued with doubt, but strangely he also sensed Mary was telling the truth. He knew Mary was a young woman of honor, and he wanted to be a man of honor. Neither she nor he had ever lied, and who could make up such a story? We can imagine that he might have thought: *I love her—but the Torah, the Law! What will happen to her if I call off this marriage? I will never forgive myself if they hurt her. Baruch Adonai, Blessed are you, Holy One, Compassionate One, do not abandon me in my time of need. I am an ordinary man and I do not know what you see in me that you would entrust your Chosen One to me. Do not keep silent but hear and answer me.*

In the end, after intense deliberation, Joseph decided to marry and then dismiss Mary quietly so as not to expose her to public disgrace. As soon as he resolved to do this, God whispered to Joseph through the voice of an angel in a dream. When he awoke, he was no longer afraid of the new path God asked him to take.

Perhaps the next day, as Mary gathered herbs in the field, Joseph suddenly approached her and repeated the words the angel had spoken to him in a dream. He would take Mary for his wife; he would not denounce her. He understood.

This is a love story. A story that is part of our heritage as adopted sisters and brothers of the unborn baby in this account. Mary would have been aware of the severe consequences and public humiliation she would endure because of her pregnancy outside of marriage. This was part of her cultural and religious heritage. We know this also because in the Scriptures Jesus saves an adulterous woman from certain death by stoning. When it came to the interpretation of the law, punishment was swift and inflexible in first-century Palestine. In the Matthean account, the words, "Her husband Joseph, being a righteous man and unwilling to expose her to public disgrace, planned to dismiss her quietly," speak volumes about the character of this gentle man. We learn about the harsh realities of antiquity concerning shame and honor. "Public disgrace" is a polite way of saying "life-threatening penalty." Joseph would have been intimately aware of the grave danger of their situation. He could have said "no," but in his "yes," he chose to save Mary's life not only out of righteousness but also out of love for her. He is a good Jew and believes that his God will be faithful and not abandon him in his time of need.

I never tire of this love story because it touches me deeply at the core of my heart. I imagine and reflect upon the extraordinary struggles of these two ordinary people, and I take courage in their trust in God's plan for them. Twenty years ago, I stood on a similar precipice that shocked me out of the ordinary and catapulted me into that place called uncertainty. My husband was diagnosed with metastatic brain cancer and given three months to live. I was thirty-two years old. Everything I knew, thought I knew, and wanted to know evaporated in that moment. While Alan was in surgery, the doctors not holding out much hope for his survival, I resisted, I struggled.

Then in the waiting room at the hospital, my hospital where I had worked as a registered nurse for four years, I experienced a wondrous event. It can only be described as a deeply spiritual experience in which all my reactions and my unformed and unspoken questions were answered. Like a near-death experience, I watched as my life from childhood through adulthood, including the present reality, unfolded like billows of textured fabric. "Why?" I seemed to be asking silently. In that dream-like state, these words engraved themselves upon my mind, heart, and soul: "Everything that you have lived through was to prepare you for this moment." I knew I could go through this experience without knowing the outcome or the twists and turns this journey would take. I felt God's love for me through the ministrations of my family, friends, colleagues, and acquaintances. My prayer throughout that horrific day was: "Lord, I pray only for the knowledge of your will for me and the strength to carry that out." Over and over I repeated that prayer like a mantra, sometimes in desperation, sometimes with hope. No bargaining, no deals or empty promises...just that simple prayer and my sorrow—that's all I had to offer to God.

I understand intimately what Mary might have felt in accepting God's challenging gift. For I see God's hand in my life in surprising and unexpected moments. I too made a rapid transition that day. In an instant, that day robbed me of my naiveté, ended my placidness, my *acedia,* and motivated me to seek a more spiritual, creative focus for my life.

Like Joseph, I knew my life would never again be the same. Dreams of children or a life together into retirement vanished. In fact, this experience robbed me of my ability to dream for many years. Just as the words "public disgrace" implied certain outcomes, so the words "cancer...only three months to live" bulged with innumerable strata of outcomes. As a nurse, these words struck terror in me as I recalled patients undergoing chemotherapy and radiation treatments. I envisioned the long road of endless visits to doctors, blood tests, pronouncements, remissions, and relapses that would invade our lives ruthlessly without mercy. Those few words released every fear I had ever known.

Yes, my life as I knew it disintegrated and I felt my soul imploding. Past, present, and future fused together seamlessly without beginning or end. Uncertainty became a way of life: familiar, less fearful, and tolerable. Eventually, I was able to befriend the uncertainty when I stopped trying to control it. But God is faithful to God's people, and I can now see that event as a springboard for everything up to and including that moment. My husband survived his cancer (that is another story!), as did I. And in this experience, I received the courage to give birth to myself, the self I was meant to be.

Love has many faces within a marriage and undergoes many changes because life's journeys—full of well-placed interruptions, winding, dusty trails, moments of peril, and treacherous turns—defy complacency. Mary and Joseph made such a journey to Bethlehem, and later, as a tiny family with the Child Jesus, into Egypt. Within the challenge of facing cancer, and definitely because of it, Alan and I were able to forge a new relationship, just as the challenges presented to Mary and Joseph caused them to reflect deeply on the new path God asked them to take. Through change and transition, we are presented with opportunities to take a risk and become midwives, with God, to our stories. Moreover, the dynamism of conversion mercifully pierces our boredom in unimaginable, wondrous, and unexpected ways when we need it the most. We can look to Mary and Joseph and see ourselves through their struggles. Enriched by their love for each other and God's love for them, they were able to go forward into the land of uncertainty without fear or misgiving. Just as the Angel Gabriel's announcement launched Mary and Joseph into a life journey in which they had to learn to embrace the unknown, Alan's diagnosis with cancer was the beginning of a life-altering journey for both of us that continues day by day.

My most precious provision for the journey is God's abundant love. How could it be anything else?

To Ponder

- How is your faith like Mary's? Like Joseph's?

- Have you ever experienced poverty in your life? How did this change you in relation to God and others?

- How is love present in your daily life? How do you show love in action?

- What place do love, the unknown, and God have in your life? Do you think of them together, as part of a single journey of life, or as separate paths? Why?

CHAPTER 7

Mary's Journey
to Bethlehem

MARÍA DE LOURDES RUIZ SCAPERLANDA has been married to Michael A. Scaperlanda for twenty-five years, and she is the proud mother of Christopher, Anamaría, Rebekah, and Michelle. She has a B.A. in journalism from the University of Texas, Austin, and an M.A. in English from the University of Oklahoma. She is the author of several books, including *The Seeker's Guide to Mary* (Loyola Press, 2002), *The Journey: A Guide for the Modern Pilgrim* (Loyola Press, 2004), and her latest, *The Complete Idiot's Guide to Mary of Nazareth* (Penguin/Alpha, 2006).

In those days a decree went out from Emperor Augustus that all the world should be registered. This was the first registration and was taken while Quirinius was governor of Syria. All went to their own towns to be registered. Joseph also went from the town of Nazareth in Galilee to Judea, to the city of David called Bethlehem, because he was descended from the house and family of David. He went to be registered with Mary, to whom he was engaged and who was expecting a child.

LUKE 2:1–5

❧

AS I GROW OLDER, I HAVE LEARNED that joy and suffering are inherently intertwined, not in the way oil and vinegar coexist in one bottle, but, rather, in the way there can be sunshine and rain in a single moment.

A son getting married and moving away. Dropping off a youngest daughter at college in a city fourteen hours away from home. Graduating and starting the next step in your education. Visiting your aging grandparents—or parents. I've heard these moments described as bittersweet. But I think there's something more, something deeper. What can we call those moments where joy and suffering literally coexist, where we are smiling while grieving—or laughing while weeping?

The Scripture passage describing the journey of Mary and Joseph from Nazareth to Bethlehem relates one of those moments in Mary's life.

As we read in the New Testament and see played out for us in *The Nativity Story,* Mary is engaged to Joseph, a descendant of the family of David. An angel comes to her and announces that she is to conceive a child—by the Holy Spirit—who will be the Son of God. She is a virgin, yet pregnant; she is having a child, but not of the man to whom she is engaged. She can feel a very human child within her womb, while she ponders in her heart what it means that he's the Son of the Most High and that she is pregnant when she is not supposed to be.

I wouldn't have blamed Mary if she felt like Job. The angel's message and what followed were "mixed good news" at best!

Yet Luke's story continues, adding hardship to the mystery. The Roman Emperor Augustus decreed that a census of the entire world should take place, specifically requiring that every man register in his hometown. Now we envision a very pregnant Mary making the ninety-mile journey with Joseph from Nazareth in

Galilee to the city of David's birth, the town of Bethlehem of Judea. They traveled on a rough trail, over ridges and through valleys, that could have taken them as long as a week by foot.

A mere five miles south of Jerusalem, the city of Bethlehem is set in the beautiful hill country. With an altitude of 2,350 feet, the area tends to be rainy in the winter—which is exactly how it was on my first visit to Israel. I walked in the rain through the steep streets thinking about how difficult the walk must have been for Mary and Joseph, especially as they entered the hill country, no doubt with crowds of people traveling alongside them and wet weather to complicate their journey.

Yes, I imagine Mary must have wondered at least some of the time, "How much more will you ask of me, Lord?" But simply touching her round belly or feeling the kicks of the beautiful son within her womb would have immediately made her smile with joy.

Indeed, this was the case with me during the "journey" of each of my four pregnancies.

Something incredible happened as I neared the end of each of my pregnancies. The child within me took up a lot of room and often made his or her presence known by kicking me in the ribs and making me sit up—or "suggesting" that I try a new position by pushing one or more organs out of place. It may sound painful, and sometimes it was. But it makes me smile to remember just how amazing it felt to have a child within me, to feel a life existing with me and within me—like when my not-yet-born baby had the hiccups!

Motherhood affects the very fabric of a person, and Mary experienced this transformation the same way any woman does when she becomes a mother. Like a life-changing makeover, it affected and altered me at every level: physically, mentally, and spiritually.

Not only was my physical appearance modified forever by pregnancy and childbirth, but there was also an invisible and undeniable mark left in my spirit by each pregnancy experience. Nothing less than a miracle of life took place within my body. A human life, known by God the Most High even before the moment of conception, was born of me, through me, making me at once and forever a mother.

Pregnancy itself is a pilgrimage journey like no other. As a mother of one boy and three girls, I can bear witness that, although we recognize each newborn child as unique and different, this is already and especially evident in pregnancy. Speaking without words, this new human life communicates his or her uniqueness to the rest of the world in every conceivable way.

I don't have scientific data outlining why or how this is so. But I know that what I experienced with each of my children inside the womb was a reflection of their unique personality traits already in motion. With each child, I felt something new. I "carried" each child differently in my body. My energy level varied, and so did my appetite. Each child was active inside the womb at different times of day—and each had different levels of activity. I could not get enough sleep when I was pregnant with my son. Yet with my next pregnancy, I had enough energy to do house projects *and* go to an exercise class three times a week! With my middle daughter, the only nourishment that sounded appetizing was Chinese food—and to this day, that's her favorite type of food.

Much in the same way, Mary knew Jesus as only a mother can know and experience the child she carries within her womb—and she shares this exceptional experience of pregnancy and motherhood with me.

In her characteristically practical and charming way, St. Thérèse of Lisieux explained in one of her letters how she envisioned the very human life of the Blessed Virgin Mary:

> It is easy to deduce that her life both in Nazareth and later on was quite ordinary. Everything took place as things occur in our own lives. The Blessed Virgin is sometimes pictured as if she were unapproachable.... She lived a life of faith common to all of us and we should prove this from what we are told in the pages of the Gospel. The Blessed Virgin is the Queen of heaven and earth, quite true, but she is more mother than queen.

More mother than queen! As St. Thérèse empha-
sizes, we can relate to Mary in a personal way because
Mary walked a very human journey.

What kind of baby would Jesus have been within
Mary's womb? From what we know of our Lord, I can
easily imagine he was an active one! But we also know
that amid his teaching, healings, and miracles, Jesus
made a point of going to an out-of-the-way place to
pray. He no doubt spent long periods inside Mary's
womb simply resting in God's care.

I also picture Mary feeling healthy and energetic
during her pregnancy, although it must have been very
uncomfortable to make the journey to Bethlehem, traveling over rocky terrain and looking for opportunities
to stretch and rest. *The Nativity Story* imagines Mary
falling off a donkey and threatened by a snake as she
and Joseph crossed a river, adding peril to discomfort.
During her journey, I imagine Mary must have tried to
eat as healthy as possible with the meager food available
to a couple as poor as she and Joseph were. There is an
especially touching scene in *The Nativity Story* that
shows how scarce food must have been for them. In it
Joseph witnesses a beast of burden falling from weakness, and he shares his own bread with the donkey carrying Mary.

As any mother will verify, Mary would have been
particularly concerned to do everything as well as she
knew how for the baby growing within her.

To be able to relate to Mary as a woman and a mother is one of the greatest gifts that God has given to women as a part of the mystery of the Incarnation.

The Nativity Story once again demonstrates how difficult it must have been for Mary, human like ourselves, to be an unwed and unexpectedly pregnant young woman yet still trust in God's plan for her life. Films can often help us on life's journey, offering us inspiration along with insight about our human condition. *The Nativity Story* can help us to relate to Mary's human joy, suffering, and hope. We can feel Mary's awe and joy as the child grows within her—and her concern as she travels to Bethlehem to give birth to this new life.

As Mary felt him move within, she must have wondered about her Son. Would he be an active, physical boy, or a quiet and reflective one? Would he smile a lot, cry a lot, or be easy to content? Would he be a morning person, a late night owl, or both? How would the mystery of his life be played out?

We can imagine her sense of hope as she and Joseph spoke about the future for the child in her womb, and we can easily conceive the expectant parents' concern about how well they could bring up such a unique and extraordinary child. As Mary says to Joseph during their journey in *The Nativity Story,* "How do we raise such a child?" Mary is reassured that Joseph will do his best as a husband and foster father to Jesus when she notices his worn, torn, and bloodied feet: the result of walking many miles, which he had done without complaining. God entrusted her well-being—and that of her Son—to a good man.

On one level, the uncertain journey that Mary and Joseph began as they traveled from Nazareth to Bethlehem was a physical metaphor for the journey that began when Mary became pregnant. With that first "yes" to the Angel Gabriel at the Annunciation, Mary became the first to welcome Jesus into her life, to acknowledge him as the Son of God; Elizabeth, another mother miraculously pregnant, was the second.

True, Mary carried the Lord, the Son of God, in her womb, yet, as St. Augustine says of the Blessed Virgin Mary, "she conceived him in her heart before she conceived him in the flesh." In this respect, Mary once again shows us the way in the spiritual and individual journey of our relationship with God our creator.

As the mother of an awesome foursome, I can easily relate to the image and the symbolism of Mary being "pregnant with God." This powerful concept of allowing God to be born within us through Mary of Nazareth is at the essence of our identity as Christians.

Like Mary, each of us is invited to acknowledge that beyond our original decision to follow Christ, there will continue to be unforeseen events, choices, and circumstances that require us to renew our commitment. Much in the same way that it can be consoling to realize, for example, that all married couples will continue to find experiences that will necessitate the renewal of their marriage vows in small, daily, concrete ways, so must we be consoled by continuing to choose Christ in the details of our everyday lives.

It is beautiful and helpful to realize that Mary was the first disciple to experience the reality of renewing her commitment to God when things were difficult. She can, therefore, both encourage and console us in our daily struggles.

God desires for us to realize and experience this truth: We are, indeed, pregnant with Love; Christ is already present within us. And as we grow and develop spiritually, we slowly come to grasp this spiritual pregnancy—this personal and individual gift of the Incarnation—as well as what it means for us, in ever-deeper ways.

As my husband, Michael, is fond of saying, thankfully this mystery unfolds before us in small steps, in God's time, so as not to overwhelm us. God does not lead us immediately from total darkness to perfect light. Such a sudden change would undoubtedly blind us. In his infinite mercy, God allows Christ to be birthed in the world—and in each of our hearts!—in a way analogous to the rising of the sun, allowing the pupils of our souls the time to adjust as the light continues to grow.

None of us has a perfect understanding of what it means to be a follower of Christ, and neither did Mary as she and Joseph journeyed toward Bethlehem. The Angel Gabriel's revelation that her Son was to be the Son of God who would reign forever must have seemed unbelievable. Her Son was to be the Messiah? And what did Mary think when Elizabeth said to her, reinforcing this almost incomprehensible notion: "And why has this happened to me, that the mother of my Lord comes to me?" (Lk 1:43)

The questions in Mary's heart must have been the same as ours now when we experience sudden and unprecedented events in our lives: How could this be? What does this mean for me, for my family? And how will I be able to make it through this?

Although she knew Jesus more intimately than we do, Mary shares with every one of us the tribulations of having this kind of personal walk of faith with the Lord. Like us, she experienced doubts and confusion, the pain and heartache of life, and ultimately confident trust in salvation and eternal life.

Mary's response when faced with the inconceivable was that lovely and honest "yes"—not because she knew something we don't know, but because she genuinely trusted God and belonged to God with her whole heart, mind, and being. Our Mother Mary was able to do this because it was enough for her to say "yes" to the moment, to the present reality, in spite of not knowing what it all would mean for the future.

Like Mary, we don't have to say "yes" to everything at once. When we consciously strive to be present to each moment, all we have to say "yes" to is right now, opening ourselves to God for the next step of our journey to our Bethlehem...wherever that might be.

To Ponder

- The author quotes St. Thérèse as saying that we can relate to Mary not because she is a queen, but because she walked a human journey like us. Do you agree? Why?

- If you are a mother, what was your experience of waiting and expectation?

- Like Elizabeth, have you ever felt truly blessed by the visit of someone you did not expect? And like Mary, how often have you visited someone with the hope of bringing that person comfort, joy, and help without expecting anything in return?

- What mysteries have unfolded in your life, and what have they meant to you? How have they changed you? Inspired you to charity?

CHAPTER 8

Mary's Journey through Fear and Doubt

Marianne Lorraine Trouvé, FSP, has been a member of the Daughters of St. Paul since 1976. She has carried out the Pauline mission of evangelization in the United States and Canada. Since 1994, she has served as an editor in the publishing house, Pauline Books & Media, in Boston. She has an M.A. in theology with a Marian concentration from the University of Dayton.

An angel of the Lord appeared to Joseph in a dream and said, "Get up and take the child and his mother, and flee to Egypt, and remain there until I tell you; for Herod is about to search for this child to destroy him."

MATTHEW 2:13

∞

MARY LIVED IN A VIOLENT WORLD. Scenes from *The Nativity Story* show Herod's soldiers in Bethlehem battering down doors. They wield their swords as the wails and screams of tormented mothers pierce the night. Not long after, the scene shifts. Tax collectors roam through the village of Nazareth demanding payment from the poor people of the land. One desperate family can't pay, but finds no mercy. A leering soldier drags their daughter off into slavery—or worse.

Living in such a world, her country under foreign occupation, Mary certainly had much to fear. Daily life meant a struggle for survival, and people often tottered on the brink between life and death. But despite this, as a daughter of Israel, Mary found courage and hope by trusting in God. She certainly would have prayed the psalms as she heard them read in her synagogue. "The LORD is my light and my salvation; whom shall I fear? The LORD is the stronghold of my life; of whom shall I be afraid?" (Ps 27:1)

I wonder if those words flew across Mary's mind on the day the Angel Gabriel appeared to her with a mission from God—a mission impossible! God invited her to be the mother of his Son, to give birth to a child conceived in a virginal way. She asked a question: "How shall this be, since I am a virgin?" The angel replied, "The Holy Spirit will come upon you, and the power of the Most High will overshadow you; therefore the child to be born will be holy; he will be called Son of God." Mary accepted the invitation. Offering herself to God, she responded, "Here am I, the servant of the Lord; let it be with me according to your word" (Lk 1:34, 35, 38). What about Joseph? She trusted that God would make it clear to him.

But Mary faced great difficulty. Did she tremble to think of how Joseph and her relatives might react when they saw her body swell as the baby grew? The movie portrays the anguish she must have felt. Mary had much to fear in a society where an unmarried pregnant woman could be stoned to death. The fear of rejection, of being cast out, must have struck her heart deeply. That mysterious sword Simeon spoke of when she brought Jesus to the Temple years later had already begun to pierce her heart: "This child is destined...to be a sign that will be opposed so that the inner thoughts of many will be revealed—and a sword will pierce your own soul too" (Lk 2:34–35).

Those words "that the inner thoughts of many will be revealed" have always intrigued me. What do they mean? In a mysterious way they may indicate that Jesus would draw forth great devotion from some people and great opposition from others. Mary would feel great sorrow as she saw others oppose her son. That grief would pierce her mother's heart like a sword, also somehow revealing "the inner thoughts of many." We might find a hint of this by imagining the reactions of people of Mary's village when she arrived home obviously pregnant. In the film, Joseph dreams that some of the townspeople pick up stones and condemn her as a sinner. Even her parents doubt her. But Joseph, despite his agony, refuses to accuse her. The characters' reactions to Mary's pain reveal their inner selves: her neighbors' self-righteous thoughts, her parents' uncertainty, and Joseph's goodness. Joseph was a just man; even as the sword pierced Mary's heart, that same sword opened his own. He listened to the word of the Lord that came to him through Gabriel: "Joseph, son of David, do not fear to take Mary as your wife, for the child conceived in her is from the Holy Spirit" (Mt 1:20).

What does Mary teach us here? In the family discussion portrayed in the movie, Mary states simply, "I have told the truth. Whether you believe is your choice, not mine." Mary listened to the angel and believed the message she heard came from God. She let God's truth into her heart, and it became her own truth. She rested secure in God's love; she didn't focus on what others thought. Even when people didn't believe her words, she stood her ground and refused to allow them to strip her of her dignity. Instead, she focused on what God had said to her heart through the angel. She listened to that still, small voice (see 1 Kings 19:12) God uses to whisper into our hearts love, strength, and support. Steadfast in God's love, Mary could withstand other people's efforts to drag her down. Although the situation caused her pain, she knew God loved and valued her—and only that mattered. She understood that other people's disbelief didn't change the truth of her situation, and she kept on going, doing what God had asked of her despite the opposition she found.

At times all of us face opposition and discouragement. Self-doubt often trips us up more than any external force. The temptation to reject ourselves, perhaps even hate ourselves, can loom up and strangle us like a snake coiling around its prey. Rejecting ourselves, we more easily reject other people. And, paradoxically, when we accept ourselves and love ourselves in the right way, we can also love and accept other people.

In difficult situations, everything hinges on which voices we choose to listen to: those that put us down or

those that build us up. *The Nativity Story* portrays Mary
and Joseph journeying to Bethlehem late in Mary's
pregnancy. They pass an elderly shepherd sitting by the
roadside in front of a flickering fire. He doesn't look at
them, but somehow he understands. In his gruff way,
he speaks a word of hope. Almost as if God revealed it
to him, he tells Mary that each of us has a gift and that
her gift is what she carries inside herself. The baby
about to be born is her gift. Just as Mary listened to
God's voice speaking to her through the angel, she lis-
tens to it speaking through the elderly shepherd.

I recall one occasion when God's voice came to me
from an unexpected source. A few years ago when I visited my family for vacation, my brother Paul took me
and my mother to see *The Sound of Music* on Broadway.
It was about eleven P.M. as we left the theater, but lights
blazed, cars honked, and people crowded the side-
walks. As we made our way through the crowd to the
parking garage, I noticed an elderly African-American
woman huddled on the sidewalk. She crouched next to
a building, warming herself near a steam grate, the
patches on her jacket fluttering in the wind. As we
went by she didn't look up but called out, "Some people
are so lucky." Did she intend those words for me? I
don't know, but those words drove straight into my
heart. In a second all sorts of feelings flooded me; I felt
sorry for her, guilty that I had eaten a steak dinner that
evening, and frustrated about a society that lets people

live on the sidewalk. She was like the shepherd, a prophet—from New York instead of Judea—who spoke God's word to me. Only God knows what kind of hand life had dealt her. That night she gave me a gift that taught me an important lesson about gratitude. Whenever I'm tempted to feel sorry for myself, those words come back to haunt me, "Some people are so lucky."

Her words also nagged at my conscience. Besides reminding me to count my blessings, they also led me to question myself about my concern for the poor. God's word is like that; it both comforts and challenges us. "Indeed, the word of God is living and active, sharper than any two-edged sword, piercing until it divides soul from spirit, joints from marrow; it is able to judge the thoughts and intentions of the heart" (Heb 4:12). Understanding how I can serve the poor is a journey of discovery for me, and I have only begun. The homeless woman made me aware of so many things, and now as I reflect theologically on this event, I pray to know what I am to do.

Not long after Jesus' birth, Mary again had great reason to fear. A power-crazed King Herod did not hesitate to shed innocent blood; he ordered his soldiers to kill all the baby boys in Bethlehem. An angel warned Joseph in a dream, and he jumped up from sleep, quickly gathered Mary and Jesus, and immediately set out for Egypt. The little family trudged along the road under the cover of night, fleeing the grave danger, refugees for the sake of the child. What did Mary feel? I can only imagine the dread that filled her heart at the thought of a soldier putting Jesus to the sword. Jesus' life was spared, but then they had to face an uncertain future as strangers in a foreign land; the sword of fear and doubt pierced Mary's heart again as she continued the journey begun at the Annunciation.

But the danger passed, and for a time Jesus was safe. Mary had many years to watch her Son grow and to take care of him, whom she loved so deeply. But another day would dawn when Simeon's words would fully come true. On Calvary, after Jesus died a most agonizing death, the Gospel of John notes that "one of the soldiers pierced his side with a spear, and at once blood and water came out" (19:35). The Gospel then quotes part of this passage:

> And I will pour out a spirit of compassion and supplication on the house of David and the inhabitants of Jerusalem, so that, when they look on the one whom they have pierced, they shall mourn for him, as one mourns for an only child, and weep bitterly over him, as one weeps over a firstborn (Zech 12:10).

On Good Friday, the sword of sorrow pierced Mary's heart as never before. As she journeyed with Jesus toward Calvary, she looked on him, her only child, and wept bitter tears. Her worst fear had come to pass. But Jesus didn't leave her bereft; before he died, he confided Mary to John, the beloved disciple, and the disciple to Mary. Then, John says, Jesus delivered over his spirit (see 19:30). Besides referring to Jesus' death, this can also refer to Jesus' gift of the Holy Spirit, whom he had promised to send after he returned to the Father. Although the apostles had fled in terror when faced with Jesus' death, Mary did not give up hope. In fact, the Church's tradition of honoring Mary on Saturday originates from the ancient belief that Mary was the only one who, after Jesus' death, never gave up hope that he would rise again.

After the resurrection and ascension, we find Mary joined in prayer with the disciples in the upper room, awaiting the promised gift of the Spirit. On Pentecost the Spirit descended on them all and filled Mary in an even richer way. At the Annunciation, the Spirit had come upon Mary and brought about the Incarnation: Jesus became a man, a human being. On Pentecost, the Spirit came upon Mary and the other disciples and brought the Church into being. The apostles, who had formerly cowered in fear behind locked doors, now boldly proclaimed Jesus to the crowds. The Holy Spirit transformed their fear into courage.

When I think about how God has helped me through doubt and fear in my own life, some major events come to mind, like my bout with cancer. But God also works in the smaller things, and one such incident carried an enormous lesson for me. When I was in seventh grade, I won the spelling bee for my school, and before I knew it, I was headed for a regional competition. My father was ecstatic. He was so proud I had won, and he dreamed that I would make it to the national bee in Washington, D.C. He realized that I first had to pass the next hurdle. So he appointed himself my Personal Spelling Coach. Every night he would drill me on word after word, finding harder ones to spring on me all the time. Part of my "training" was that I had to read five pages of the dictionary every day. After school, all my friends were outside playing while I slaved away learning words, much like the girl in the film *Akeelah and the Bee* (2006)!

At last, the great day came and I went to the regional spelling bee. Ironically, my father had to work, so I went with my mother and two nuns from my school. The competition was tough, but I was doing well. Finally only three of us remained. Tension mounted. I was asked to spell "perspiration." I began "P-I-R...." and instantly I knew I had blown it. The bell clanged. I was out. I slunk back to my seat, wondering how I would break the news to Dad. As we drove home, my mother chatted pleasantly, trying to help me put my loss in perspective and not feel too badly about it.

When I told my father the news that night, I could tell he was crushed. He felt terrible I had lost, though he didn't say much about it. On my way to my room, I realized something important. Underneath the disappointment of losing, another feeling was starting to surface: relief! No more word drills, no more reading the dictionary; I could go out and play with my friends after school. A part of me had actually feared winning, feared success because of what it might bring. I didn't really want to go to Washington to compete in the national spelling bee. By losing, I was free to be a kid again!

In other ways as my life has unfolded, I've had to contend with this same strange fear of success. It could be a lot easier to go through life not living up to my potential. I've felt the temptation to hold back, to sabotage myself at key moments so my life would be a little easier and I would face fewer demands. But that would be refusing to give the gifts I have, which are meant to be shared with others. The shepherd told Mary that her gift was what she carried inside herself, and Mary freely and joyfully gave that gift to the world. Like Mary, you and I carry gifts inside ourselves. In those moments when we're tempted to hold on to the gift instead of giving it—those pierced-heart moments—Mary can help us let go of our fears. Pope John Paul II used to speak of "the law of the gift"—which is the idea that we somehow find fulfillment by giving ourselves away. He was simply saying in a new way what Jesus taught long ago: "It is more blessed to give than to receive" (Acts 20:35).

To Ponder

- How do you see the poor? Can you hear what they are saying?

- What is one gift God has given to you? How do you share it with others?

- Jesus became a human being just like us, so it must mean that we are lovable. Do you truly love yourself? Do you believe that Christ loves you unconditionally?

- What are your fears? How can the contemplation of Mary's story in the Scriptures assuage your fears?

CHAPTER 9

Mary's Journey
of Sorrow

Marilyn Gill, a native of Panama, is a widow and the mother of five children. She attended Indiana University-Purdue University, later earning her M.A. in spiritual psychology from the University of Santa Monica. Gill has over two decades of television experience and is a member of the Television Academy of Arts and Sciences, Producers Guild, and Catholics in Media.

When Herod saw that he had been tricked by the wise men, he was infuriated, and he sent and killed all the children in and around Bethlehem who were two years old or under, according to the time that he had learned from the wise men. Then was fulfilled what had been spoken through the prophet Jeremiah:

> *"A voice was heard in Ramah,*
> *wailing and loud lamentation,*
> *Rachel weeping for her children;*
> *she refused to be consoled, because they are*
> * no more."*

MATTHEW 2:16–18

IT IS AN IMPROMPTU BABY SHOWER. Gift boxes, wrapping paper, baby booties, blankets, rattles, and cards are strewn across the red Formica table, ribbons dangling off its stainless steel edge. "It's so cute!" I squeal. I take the tissue-encased gift out of the box and shake off the paper, pulling out a yellow baby gown. Holding it up, I show it to the five other teenage girls squeezed into the tiny kitchen of the home I've grown up in. "I got yellow, since we don't know if you're having a girl or a boy," explains Carmella.

"I can't believe you're not going to be in the music festival this year," states another girl. "It's going to be weird without you here."

"Remember the time you hid in library bathroom so you'd get locked in over the weekend?" my friend Lydia recalls. We all chuckle at the innocent childhood prank. Growing up without television, reading was my world beyond my world. I simply wanted to read all the time.

Someone else brings up the time in the fourth grade when I got in trouble during summer school. While all the other kids were learning how to make macramé plant hangers, Sister Loretta was reprimanding me for sitting in the back of church reading my mother's paperback copy of *Peyton Place*....

"I still can't believe you gave up your scholarship," Lydia interjects, her voice tinged with disbelief. My mother could not believe it either, especially since I had been a straight-A student aspiring to continue my studies. But falling in love and marrying one of the American soldiers stationed at the army base in Panama had definitely changed my plans.

In an effort to lighten the mood, Carmella reaches under the mound of gifts and wrapping paper to find the knob on the radio at the far end of the table. She cranks up the volume, and the Beatles' "Let It Be" bursts through, crackling with static. Carmella begins to sing the familiar words, and the five of us join in. My hand moves to my six-month pregnant belly in an effort to soothe the baby stretching and kicking inside.

Tomorrow I will leave behind my parents and friends in Panama and embark on a new life in the United States with Louie, my husband of eight months. I am excited about the journey. An image of the Holy Family flits across my mind: Joseph leading the donkey carrying his pregnant, teenaged wife, Mary. I wonder what they might have talked about on the road from Nazareth to Bethlehem. Whatever the future holds for my new family and me, I am happy and optimistic.

As we belt out the last notes of "Let It Be," the six of us hug. Although I do not realize it, those words— "When I find myself in times of trouble, Mother Mary comes to me, speaking words of wisdom, let it be"— will be the anthem for my future, the peaceful refrain of my prayer in days to come.

∝∞∝

THE 1960s LANDSCAPE OF MY CHILDHOOD was steeped in Catholic tradition and socialization, complete with soccer-playing Maryknoll nuns and chaperoned teen dances following Friday night novena. Dances were open to all teenagers, regardless of religion, and were well attended. We rocked, rolled, and salsaed to a stack of forty-fives spinning on a portable record player hooked to a couple of loud speakers. Our chaperones were a community of parents who showed up and served hot dogs and cokes. While making sure we did not get too close to our partners during the slow dances, they debated the issues of the day, touching upon politics, religion, and which numbers were the most likely winners in the national lottery. We were kept safe, and the possibility of sorrow or suffering never crossed our minds. Thinking back to the role Mary played in my life as a girl, I recall that she was always present, an accepted if largely unnoticed part of my family, worship, and culture. Only after giving birth did I find that Mary was closer to me than I had ever imagined.

After arriving in the United States and beginning to settle into my new home, I finally heard the words: "Congratulations, you have a beautiful, six-pound-ten-ounce baby girl!" With that, the nurse at the military hospital in Maryland deposited into my arms a blanket with my newborn daughter swaddled inside. The warmth of her body surprised me as I peeked inside the blanket at the tiny face looking up at me. Never having been around newborns, I marveled at her baby scent. Louie, sitting on a chair next to my bed, leaned in to get a look at our daughter. When he gently touched her impossibly small hand, the grip that tightened around his finger caught him off guard. "Whoa!" he exclaimed with delight. "She's strong!"

"Have you picked out a name for your beautiful baby girl?" the nurse asked.

Louie and I looked at each other and smiled in silent agreement. "Michelle," I answered, "like the Beatles' song."

"That's a very nice name," the nurse responded. She proceeded to give me instructions on nursing my child, then told me the doctor would be in momentarily. As if on cue, a tall man with wire-rimmed glasses entered the room. Four young, somber-looking interns trailed behind him. "I'm Major Phillips," the doctor announced. "I'm glad you're both here. I need to speak with you."

The words that followed were so terrifying that I've blocked them from memory. My husband and I listened in shocked disbelief as the doctor informed us that our precious baby girl had been diagnosed with hydrocephalus.

"What do you mean—it's nearly always fatal?" Louie asked, his voice rising with alarm. "Could it be a mistake?" Instinctively I hugged Michelle closer, as if to shelter her from the world outside. I was too stunned to cry, and I steeled myself to stay calm and alert to this doctor's every word. I kept telling myself this could not be happening, while over and over again the silent question ran through my mind: "Why, God, why?" The doctor was speaking in what seemed like a foreign language. I heard snatches: "the circumference of her head will continue to enlarge...it's unlikely that she'll survive past...decreased mental function." I touched the scapular hanging around my neck; on its front was a picture of the Immaculate Heart of Mary. "Is there a chapel in this hospital?" I asked.

The eight weeks that followed—in which our daughter remained hospitalized—were extremely difficult for Louie and me. We were both so young. Each suffering, we hardly knew how to comfort the other, and communication between us was strained. There were days when I thought of the Holy Family and wondered how Joseph must have felt when he first realized Mary was having a baby he was unable to explain. His dilemma is clearly shown in *The Nativity Story*. He must have grappled with what people were saying behind his back. Louie, too, wondered what people might say about the challenges we would have to face with *our* baby. He reacted to the pressure by immersing himself in work. For my part, I began an uninterrupted dialogue with Mary, turning to her at every moment for strength and support for the painful journey my family had begun. She and Joseph were also young when they set out on a journey that would contain joy along with its share of sorrow.

For the first time, I fully comprehended why the image of the Immaculate Heart of Mary is surrounded with thorns. I'd always known the thorns to be a symbol of the piercing pain a mother experiences when she loses a child, but now I understood the image in a way that was frighteningly real and intimate. I was terrified I might lose my child or that she would face a life of severe limitations. Yet thinking of Mary somehow helped me to deal with the worry and fear.

What struck me most during this period was Mary's incredible ability to show grace during trying times in her life as a young mother. *The Nativity Story* depicts Mary's numerous difficulties: pregnancy outside of marriage; a journey to Bethlehem that must have been incredibly uncomfortable for a woman in the latter stages of pregnancy; giving birth in a smelly, dirty stable without any women to help her. In *The Nativity Story,* Mary expresses a serenity that I could only yearn for as an anxious young mother. What peace I was able to find, what grace I was able to show, I believe came to me through her intercession. I prayed the Rosary often during those days, not actually thinking about the words, but hanging on for dear life. I prayed and somehow remained hopeful. And I never stopped believing in miracles.

At the time of my daughter's surgery, the procedure the doctors used was still in its early stages of development. A blessed and wonderfully skilled neurosurgeon at Walter Reed Medical Center in Washington, D.C., fitted my eight-week-old daughter with a shunt, a device inserted into her skull to divert and drain the excess fluid surrounding her brain. Once the procedure was completed, the doctors attempted to gauge the operation's success, performing dozens of tests; it was now even more difficult to leave our newborn in the hospital.

Finally, a month after surgery, we brought home our three-month-old daughter, her shaved and swollen head covered with bandages. Throughout the following days and weeks, I continued to contemplate Mary's obedience and trust. She displayed such courage and faith when faced with circumstances beyond her control. Mary showed me by example to surrender, to trust in my God and his care for the future well-being of my child.

Now, thirty years later, my daughter Michelle is a beautiful, healthy young woman leading a full, active life and working as an artist and a real estate agent.

Although I have experienced other sorrows along the way—my husband died very young and I later lost a twenty-two-year-old son to accidental death—Mary's example has always sustained me on my journey. One line in particular from her Magnificat speaks to me: *"My soul magnifies the Lord, and my spirit rejoices in God my Savior, for he has looked with favor on the lowliness of his servant."* With Mary's help, in times of joy—and particularly in those times of sorrow—I have learned to "let it be."

To Ponder

- Mary grew up in a family and a village that placed God at the center of everything; is God the central point of your life? How so?

- What do you do when sorrow crosses your path? How is God present in that?

- In the sad moments of life, how might it help to reflect on the experiences of people from the Bible and how their faith sustained them?

- Read the Book of Psalms, perhaps choosing to pray with one psalm a day. While reading, listen to the emotions of sorrow, anger, rejoicing, hope, and thankfulness being expressed and think about the people who uttered these words, their familiarity with God, the Creator of us all.

CHAPTER 10

Mary's Journey into the Unknown

MARY KATHLEEN GLAVICH, SND, a Sister of Notre Dame from Cleveland, Ohio, is a pastoral associate at St. Dominic Parish. She has served as a teacher and an author/editor for several textbook series. Her latest books are the award-winning *The Confirmed Catholic's Companion* (ACTA Publications) and *A Crash Course in Teaching Religion* (Twenty-Third Publications). Glavich has a B.A. from Notre Dame College of Ohio and an M.A. in Secondary Education from the University of Minnesota. She is currently writing a book about Mary for ACTA Publications.

When Herod died, an angel of the Lord suddenly appeared in a dream to Joseph in Egypt and said, "Get up, take the child and his mother, and go to the land of Israel, for those who were seeking the child's life are dead." Then Joseph got up, took the child and his mother, and went to the land of Israel. But when he heard that Archelaus was ruling over Judea in place of his father Herod, he was afraid to go there. And after being warned in a dream, he went away to the district of Galilee. There he made his home in a town called Nazareth, so that what had been spoken through the prophets might be fulfilled, "He will be called a Nazorean."

MATTHEW 2:19–23

∞

JUST AS CLASSIC ANCIENT HEROES like Ulysses were tested on journeys, saints are tested by God. Mary, the Mother of God, was no exception. You would think that giving birth in a stable among strangers in a strange town was challenge enough. But soon after that, Mary's life journey took another unexpected turn that required heroic courage and trust.

The Gospel of Matthew skillfully relates the story, which both fulfills the prophecy "Out of Egypt I have called my son" (Mt 2:15) and parallels Jesus' life with the life of the great hero Moses. As an infant in Egypt, Moses was rescued from Pharaoh's slaughter of Hebrew male babies. Moses' survival enabled God—through him—to lead the Chosen People out of slavery and into the Promised Land. According to Matthew, while the Holy Family was still in Bethlehem, one night Joseph awakened Mary. He said, "In a dream an angel told me to flee with you and the baby to Egypt. Herod is about to search for Jesus to kill him." Mary sat up, her heart pounding with fear for her Son.

Now, after the shock, Mary could have responded, "It was just a dream, Joseph. Go back to sleep," or, "Let's wait until morning when we can see," or, "Why don't we take a few days to discern this? We can consult the local rabbi," or, "Egypt? That's about a three-day journey—an unwise move for a newborn." Mary also could have complained to God, "How could you do this to us? Haven't we gone through enough? This is no way to treat your Son." Instead, attuned to God's will, she sprang into action. She helped Joseph pack their few things, mounted the donkey, and carefully took her baby from Joseph's hands. The three of them ventured into the darkness, into the unknown. They had only the stars to guide them, and they were alone; this time, no caravan gave protection and guidance.

Instead of returning home to Nazareth, the young couple headed to a foreign land, where there was a Jewish community—but no family or friends. Mary probably wept. Maybe Jesus and Joseph did, too.

Along the way a thousand questions must have tormented Mary like pesky mosquitoes: *How will we know the way? Will we be able to get food? Where will we live? Will Joseph find work? Will I ever see my mother and father again?* And most important: *Will we be able to keep Jesus safe from the murderous King Herod?* Mary, like us, couldn't see the future. Just when she thought her life was about to return to normal and she would be somewhat in control, Mary's safe, comfortable world was shattered once more. Again she had to surrender to new occurrences and abandon herself to God's love and mercy.

Apocryphal Gospels tell charming tales about the journey to Egypt: fierce beasts came and adored the Baby Jesus, palm trees bent down to give the Holy Family dates, robbers were awed by the royal infant and turned away, and the trip was miraculously shortened. Numerous shrines in Egypt are tributes to these miracles. But Matthew's simple words offer no reason to think the escape into Egypt was eased by supernatural events. We can assume that the three travelers suffered heat, dirt, fatigue, and hunger, just as we would have.

In the crypt of the Basilica of the National Shrine of the Immaculate Conception in Washington, D.C., there is a touching sculpture by Anna Hyatt Huntington: "The Holy Family Resting: The Flight into Egypt." One of my favorite pieces of art, it portrays Mary, Joseph, Jesus, and the donkey sound asleep. The description explains that the sculpture represents the Holy Family "struggling, against great obstacles, to foster family life and preserve their faith in a loving and merciful God." Mary dominates the scene, a tower of strength and calm even as her faith is tested.

Seated atop the donkey and rocked by its gentle movement, Mary must have longed to go faster to distance her baby from the swords of Herod's soldiers. She would have strained to hear if the sound of their horses' galloping hooves were coming nearer and nearer. She would have glanced behind now and then to see if they were approaching. Mary's imagination probably tormented her, flashing horrible scenes in her mind. Her heart must have been heavy with disturbing thoughts: *How can this be? If my child is the Son of God, why are these terrible things happening to us? Maybe I was just imagining that an angel spoke to me. What if we don't save his life?*

Because Mary was the woman who had sung the Magnificat, no doubt she drew strength from its words based on Hebrew Scripture: "He has brought down the powerful from their thrones, and lifted up the lowly" (Lev 1:52). She trusted that the mighty Herod would be vanquished somehow and that her people, oppressed by the Romans occupying their land, would triumph—in particular, her Son.

When the little family stopped at the side of the road to rest, Mary would have taken out the bread, cheese, and fruit she had hastily packed and share it with Joseph. She would have nursed her baby boy, perhaps singing a song that Jewish mothers sang to their babies. Looking lovingly at the tiny face and hands of the infant in her arms, Mary surely pondered what else might be in store for him, herself, and Joseph.

All of us at certain moments in life find ourselves in Mary's position on the night of the flight to Egypt. Unexpectedly we are called to plunge into unknown territory. Maybe your spouse suddenly asks for a divorce, or you lose your job. Maybe you are called to do volunteer work in a foreign country or walk with someone nearing death. No matter what the detour and how great the shock, we can look to Mary as a model of courage and trust in God's loving care. And like her, we will be sustained by the presence of her Son, Jesus, as well as God's word in Scripture...and a friend or two.

In my life there have been two major occasions when I could identify with Mary as she fled into a foreign land. One was entering the convent barely a month after my eighteenth birthday. Driving there with my family, I cried the whole way, and my mother said she felt as if she were taking me to kindergarten again. Entering prior to the changes of Vatican II, I experienced a novitiate comparable to military boot camp. The life was quite different from how I had pictured it. While I had envisioned having a lovely time living with the sisters who had been my teachers, a community tradition prevented us newcomers from speaking to them. Every day we discovered a new challenge: we could only see our family six times a year—and only when they came to the convent to visit; we could receive mail only on Sunday, but not during Advent or Lent; we couldn't read the newspaper or watch TV; and we performed acts of humility and penance I thought had disappeared with the Middle Ages. The worst part for me was that the year I entered, many of the teachers I had looked up to and loved left the convent. As the weeks turned into months, I began to wonder if I really belonged here.

One day I was in chapel praying, "What should I do?" when, on impulse, I walked up to the open Bible near the altar. My eyes fell on the verse, "And everyone who has left houses or brothers or sisters or father or mother or children or fields, for my name's sake, will receive a hundredfold, and will inherit eternal life" (Mt 19:29). I felt that God was speaking to me through Scripture, reassuring me. And I stayed.

I imagine that on the way to Egypt, Mary found comfort in praying verses such as, "The LORD is my light and my salvation; whom shall I fear?" (Ps 27:1), and, "You show me the path of life" (Ps 16:11). She must have constantly replayed in her heart Gabriel's prophetic words about her Son and his kingdom, using the memory to motivate herself to ride out the circumstances, as puzzling and frustrating as they were.

Just as Mary spoke her initial "yes" to God, I said "yes" when I crossed the convent threshold. But just as Mary did, I have had to renew that first yes over and over again. Often what I've been asked to do as a religious has made as much sense to me as being told to go to Egypt! I could provide multiple examples of journeys that have taken me by surprise, but in all cases I survived and even thrived because, as Mary found, you "get grace" to do what you must. God is truly Emmanuel, "God with us."

Another major leap into the unknown happened when I herniated a disk. The sports doctor who diagnosed me explained that this often happens to women with "giraffe-like" necks. (A friend commented, "He *could* have said 'swan-like'!") The excruciating shoulder pain drove me into a foreign world of doctors, therapy rooms, and hospitals. Finally, after an MRI, a risky double surgery was recommended to repair my spine. After praying over the options, I decided to go ahead with it.

Just as Mary was given Joseph—a good, loving man—to journey with her as she lived out her mission, so during the days before my surgery God sent people to minister to me in different ways. A stranger whom another sister had met came to visit and walked me through the process, which she had undergone herself. Because I had no primary care doctor to give me the needed clearance for the surgery, my surgeon's nurse gave me the name of her family doctor. Before I left for the hospital, my spiritual director was there to anoint and pray with me.

I remember lying on my back under a tree the day before surgery, looking at the sky through the branches and thinking how my life was truly in the balance. It was a strange feeling to face the unknown and realize I was not in control of my life. Anything could happen in the operating room. I prayed, "Here I am. Whatever will be, I'm yours"—my own version of Mary's, "Let it be done with me according to your word" (Lk 1:38).

In the surgery room, a line from Psalm 23 crossed my mind: "Even though I walk through the valley of death..." The surgeon remarked, "Sister, you look scared." I was probably as white as the sheet that covered me. Hours later, I awoke from a successful procedure with my neck encased in a brace and a titanium plate screwed into my spine. That night in the hospital I couldn't sleep as I anxiously awaited the pain, ready to press the button to release the medication at its first hint. But the pain never came.

That day a physical therapist came to help me walk down the hall. Clutching the belt at the back of my robe, he commented on how well I was doing. I replied,

"That's because I don't have any pain." My doctor credited my easy surgery to his and his partner's skill, but I think there was more to it. That night I was transferred to my community's health care center, where I was supposed to stay for six weeks while I slowly graduated from a walker to a cane. Instead, I needed neither; three days after arriving at the center, I was sent home: an incredible close to an uncertain journey.

Because of Mary's willingness to follow God's directions to flee to Egypt, her baby survived the massacre. He lived to save the world. Sometimes, looking back on the detours in my life, I can see the blessings that came from my efforts to accept them. I met people who enriched my life, I had experiences that made me a better minister to others, and I became a stronger person. More amazing is that I often *enjoyed* the detours! My rollercoaster life has been much more exciting than the straight, steady path I had envisioned for myself.

As a Sister of Notre Dame, dedicated to Our Lady, I am heir to the same promises she had from God:

> When you pass through the waters, I will be with you;
> and through the rivers, they shall not overwhelm you;
> when you walk through fire you shall not be burned,
> and the flame shall not consume you (Is 43:2).

This gives me courage and hope for the future. Whatever it holds, I know that "all things work for good for those who love God" (Rom 8:28), as they did in the end for Mary.

To Ponder

- Have you ever had a dream or other experience in which God seemed to be speaking to you? How did you know it was God's voice?

- Mary's safety was threatened on the way to Bethlehem, yet she continued to trust that God would keep her safe. Are there times when you feel yourself threatened, and, if so, does trust play a part in your response?

- Think about a time when your life seemed out of control. Who or what kept you anchored?

- Is there a Scripture passage that speaks to you in your particular life situation?

CHAPTER 11

Mary's Journey —and Ours

M. JEAN FRISK is a member of the Secular Institute of the
Schoenstatt Sisters of Mary (www.schoenstaetter-marienschwest-
ern.org/). She holds a Licentiate in sacred theology from the
International Marian Research Institute in Dayton, Ohio, where
she is currently employed for the arts and special projects. She has
authored various articles, books, and features for "The Mary Page"
(www.udayton.edu/mary/). She has published *The Rosary of Jesus
and Mary* and *Joyous Expectation: Journeying through Advent with
Mary* with Pauline Books & Media, Boston. This is the story of her
vocation.

And the angel said to her,
"Do not be afraid, Mary."

∞

IN THE MOVIE *The Nativity Story,* screenwriter Mike Rich concludes the film with the dread command of King Herod that every baby boy under two years old be killed. The scene cuts horror into the hearts of viewers, even as the cherished melody of "Silent Night, Holy Night" overlays the hideous event with an ironic calm. Thankfully, we know the end of the story, recorded for us from the memories of the early believers. We know that Joseph and Mary escape.

Under the cover of night, Joseph guides his young wife and her child into the desert. They do not hear the screams of the mothers or see the despair of the fathers. There is no merciless rain, mud, and terror in the desert. There, with stars close enough to touch, Mary looks with amazed love into the face of her little son, and Joseph turns to her and smiles.

In his script, Mike Rich evokes Mary and Joseph's shared commitment to bring this child safely to Egypt, the land of their forefathers' exile, despite the endless desert ahead of them. We know the end of the story, but did Mary? Did Joseph? In the midst of their flight, did they know where to go? Did they try to avoid the main highways? Did they quietly wonder and whisper in the desert darkness? They were fleeing to the land intertwined with their people's history, where the language was not their own, where the Chosen People were once enslaved. Now, however, the foreign country of Egypt would be their refuge, the place where they would escape terror.

We know the end of the story, but Mary and Joseph did not. Were they anxious and afraid? Did the rolling sands of the desert swallow them, isolate them, and did they feel alone and abandoned in the vast, still darkness? The exile of Babylon, the ancient exile of Egypt that the Hebrews faced years before—and that Mary and Joseph now faced—were these *places* the real exile? Does it matter where we are when God is with us? Perhaps the couple whispered to one another in the desert night that the only apparently impenetrable exile is hatred, greed, and lust in selfish human hearts.

Mike Rich must have imagined something like this when his script allows the smile of Joseph to warm our hearts. Joseph smiles, Mary smiles, and there is hope. But in reality, when Joseph wraps his garment tightly around his shoulders to ward off the cold of a desert night, perhaps he worries, too. Where will he find work? Where will they be safe? And what does Mary wonder as she looks into the face of her baby?

As the couple walks quietly along, perhaps they sense the divine presence, remember the God of the covenant, and know he will keep his promises as he always does. They just don't know how he will do it. They know this child will deliver the peoples. Perhaps those brilliant stars in the Christmas sky remind them of the Lord who is the light to the nations and whose deliverance will never end (see Is 51:4–6).

The mystery remains; each of us must walk into the desert with Joseph, Mary, and the Child Jesus. Salvation history, the covenant story, continues in the life of every person. For us, the choices we make, the love we accept or reject, will determine the end of the story....

∞

SHE WAS SCARED. SHE WAS SLEEPING over at a friend's house for the first time in her life, sharing Judy's big bed instead of her own with her little sister. Everything was different in this house, old and creaky and cold. She turned over and cried. This wasn't fun after all, and Mama was so far away.

Morning brought something else to fear. Judy and her family were going to church. She had never been to church. Afraid again...but also curious! It was just a big hall with folding chairs, but oh, the singing! The kids went downstairs and drew pictures while someone read a story. She remembered it till she was old and gray— about Noah and all those animals, about Jesus born in a barn, to a mother named Mary. She drew an ark and a rainbow and put Mary on the boat—right in the middle, on top. Mary was holding a baby and was singing.

When Mama came to pick her up, she ran into her warm embrace and whispered, "Mama, I found out something you never told me: There's a God and he loves us!" Mama knelt down, drew her closer, and admitted through tears, "Yes, there is a God and he loves us!"

Not long after, a priest came to the farmyard gate; her Mama didn't let him in, but the next thing she knew, she was going to summer religion school for two weeks. Women wearing huge black veils and tiny faces with warm, bright eyes were teaching her about the God who loves us, about Jesus, Mary, and Joseph. She couldn't get enough—like a strange kind of hunger. She believed every word and wanted to win all of the sisters' homemade holy cards with the silky ribbons. She carefully put them in her jewelry box, but pulled them out time and time again. In the quiet of her room, she remembered the stories and looked at the pictures—Mary looked so young, so beautiful as she held Baby Jesus.

Within the space of two weeks, she was baptized, made her first confession—scared to death, not of being scolded or being bad, but of memorizing the "Act of Contrition" prayer—and received her first communion. By now she was eight and entirely in love with those gentle women in big black veils with warmth in their eyes, who told about the God who loves us and about Mary who loved God. Mary was our mother, too, and she could help us love God. We just needed to ask her.

She wondered if Mary played with other children, if she got lonesome when the wind blew, and how it was when the angel came. Mama bought her and her sister a Mary statue—plaster of Paris—but she broke off the head roughhousing in the bedroom. Her Mama glued it back together and put it on the living room mantle instead—safer there. Still, she missed having Mary in her room, with her wide-open arms reaching down to teach her about Jesus and listen to her chatter.

Her sister liked to play Indian princess in the woods, but she played church, building Mary little houses out of ferns and flowers and scraps of baby blue satin. She started talking to Mary, asking her this or that and wondering about the angel's visit. Already, she knew she was going to be a sister someday—belong to Jesus, be like Mary, teach the children. She saw it in the sunset and heard it in the wind. She devoured stories about nuns and actually *liked* the feel of the pews and the smell of incense in church!

She told a few people about her dream, and they laughed. So she decided it was her secret. She kept pulling out her holy pictures and telling Mary about her desires. There was a loneliness, a hunger that grew terrible when the wind groaned in the big pines. Beyond, beyond—she yearned for something beyond and bigger, far bigger than anything imagination could render. Sometimes she thought that this must be what love is.

She was eleven now. Her little sister played with dolls, played house, and imagined Prince Charming—sometimes as a cowboy, sometimes as a handsome wild Indian—sweeping her away. But she didn't play with dolls. As for the handsome young man, she asked Mary if it would be okay to think of Jesus sweeping her away to Africa or somewhere beyond the wind to teach everyone about the God who loves us. But that was her secret.

Suddenly, she was fifteen and terrified—her father had lost his job, and his new employment had taken them to a big city, far away from everything known and safe: the pines and the wind, the farm and the wonderful wild things. She hated her new surroundings: the crowds, the smells, the noise! Her family's upper flat—there were five children now—had no room where she could be alone and pull out her jewelry box to look at her holy cards. There was no mantle for the Mary statue with her mended neck.

She dragged her feet, pouted, made her parents sad and sometimes angry. Although she would never admit being mad at God—that might bring "consequences" —she was definitely mad at Mary.

Her new church was a big hall with scraping folding chairs. Nobody sang. It was hot and awful. It was a brand new parish with lots of screaming kids, but the pastor liked the teenagers. He invited them for a Sunday breakfast to organize religion classes. She felt that hunger again. Religion classes were interesting, and—imagine that!—there were other girls who actually talked openly about "going to the convent." They went to grottoes to pray! They joined groups for girls, went on weekends called retreats, and talked about the mysteries of the world, about the hunger for God and love and service. Talked about Mary, wanted to be like Mary! She wasn't alone!

There was a priest who spoke as if he, like Joseph, had been at Mary's side all his long life: "Think of Mary! She was probably fifteen when the angel told her she had found favor with God. Think of Mary! She was afraid! But was she afraid once she knew God loved her in such an extraordinary way? Love took wing in Mary's heart. Love overshadowed her. Her love welled up in an embracing 'yes' that has resounded throughout the ages. Was she afraid when she ran to help Elizabeth? Was she afraid on the journey to Egypt? Love conquers fear—every fear. If you know and believe you are loved, you can go anywhere, do anything, sing any song!"

She believed it was true: Mary *was* afraid at first, but she listened nonetheless. She was attentive to the voice in the wind. Even in her fear, she quietly pondered what this message might mean—to bear a Son, a child who was destined to be great. When the angel spoke, Mary reflected. She thought before she responded. What an overwhelming moment it must have been to be called *favored* of God! Love poured out and over-flowing! Love that needed an answer! Love that had consequences far beyond her tiny self! Mary, the favored one, fully overshadowed by Love personified, would bow down in worship of the God of love now dwelling within her.

And the fifteen-year-old knew somehow that this God who loved Mary had also chosen her in some odd way long ago, when she drew the ark with Mary in the middle, holding Jesus. Her heart learned a new free-dom from Mary—the freedom to embrace God's love and leave behind the terrors. Now she knew that there was a reason she had to leave the wild lake, the turf and wind—be torn from her beloved home. If she had stayed there, she would never have found the priest who shared her exile and helped her find hope, this holy man who taught that the fundamental law of the world is love. One's life and judgment of self and others, day in and day out, are measured by this unquenchable hunger to love and be loved.

Hadn't it been the same throughout history? Hadn't it been the same for Joseph and Mary on their way to Egypt with the Child Jesus?

The call to leave everything behind and embrace the Lord, no matter what the fears, is also a challenge to reach out for something—for *Someone*—far greater than self. Bearing the Son of God wasn't Mary's initiative. She couldn't possibly have dreamed this dream for herself. She was led, favored, chosen by the Spirit. Nevertheless, the answer was hers and hers alone to give—freely, wholeheartedly, faithfully. The Almighty did great things to Mary and through her. But Mary had a greatness in her own right, too! It consisted in her open readiness to serve the One—the only One—who can be called the Son of the Most High. The same can be said of Joseph, who faithfully stayed at Mary's side. He remained committed, and in his commitment he could smile.

∽

HER HAIR IS SILVER WHITE NOW. This very summer she stood again in the little church on the hill where she made her first communion. She thought of all the years in between, from the conviction of call to the present day. She remembered where the call led—to unimagined vistas, overseas countries, the challenges of living in cultures other than her own.... She recalled her secret and the gentle voices of the women in black who taught about the God who loves us. And she pictured Mary, so highly favored, on the road to Elizabeth, to Bethlehem, to Egypt, and—who knows for sure—perhaps with John to Ephesus, to Patmos. How had Mary mastered life? How had she struggled to know and understand her ongoing part in her Son's destiny? The Bible does not tell us she was visited by angels ever again. Ah, but she did have an advantage no one else has ever had! She had contained Love himself within her very body and given birth to him. And Joseph did not leave her!

Standing in the little church, the silver-haired sister remembered how much she loved Jesus there. It was there that she knew she would be a sister someday. There were times when her heart bled, when she didn't understand the Lord and his ways. She never quite got hold of that rapid-fire temper, but she learned over the years to step back and take stock. When she calmed down, she learned from Mary to ponder the Lord and trust him, no matter where the journey went. Mary's school of love for the Lord implies pondering, keeping his precious word treasured in her heart, turning fear into questions, asking him for the good wine—*for others!* Isn't that the Christian's vocation?

Long ago, the priest had told her that it's not what your job is that matters...it's how you do it. Love alone determines its value. Love alone makes the home and the workplace beautiful. Unless one lays down her life on the other side of the cross, the meaning of life remains shallow. Mary accepted Love. She stood by Love. She loved. *That* is vocation.

When presented with her vocation, Mary was counseled: *Do not be afraid!* Did she remember this in the desert on the way to Egypt? The quiet call of love is every person's hunger. It is also every person's fear. Where will my love, my service, take me? Will they accept me there, like me? Will I make it? Will I be happy? Mary answered. Joseph answered. Both left home. They were faithful, focused, committed.

The silver-haired sister looked around once more to the spot where she had knelt when she prayed: "O good Jesus, hear me, within your wounds hide me; let me never be separated from you...." And in that spot, she prayed a new prayer, a prayer Joseph and Mary must have prayed on their way to Egypt: Good Father in heaven, what's next?

To Ponder

- Have you ever been truly afraid of the future? What did you do in the face of that fear?

- What is your vocation in life? How did you know this is God's plan for you?

- In the movie *The Nativity Story,* Mary's sense of her vocation developed over time. If you had been a friend of Mary at this time in her life, what advice would you have given her?

- If you are discerning your vocation in life, write a prayer that reflects Mary's openness to God as expressed in the Scriptures.

 Rose Pacatte, fsp, is a Daughter of St. Paul and the director of the Pauline Center for Media Studies in Los Angeles, CA. She is also a noted national and international media literacy specialist, an award-winning author of books on scripture and film, and the film/TV columnist for the national Catholic magazine *St. Anthony Messenger.* She has an M.A. in Education in Media Studies from the University of London and is a frequent speaker at conferences throughout the United States and abroad.

BOOKS & MEDIA

The Daughters of St. Paul operate book and media centers at the following addresses. Visit, call or write the one nearest you today, or find us on the World Wide Web, www.pauline.org

CALIFORNIA
3908 Sepulveda Blvd, Culver City, CA 90230	310-397-8676
2460 Broadway Street, Redwood City, CA 94063	650-369-4230
5945 Balboa Avenue, San Diego, CA 92111	858-565-9181

FLORIDA
145 S.W. 107th Avenue, Miami, FL 33174	305-559-6715

HAWAII
1143 Bishop Street, Honolulu, HI 96813	808-521-2731
Neighbor Islands call:	866-521-2731

ILLINOIS
172 North Michigan Avenue, Chicago, IL 60601	312-346-4228

LOUISIANA
4403 Veterans Memorial Blvd, Metairie, LA 70006	504-887-7631

MASSACHUSETTS
885 Providence Hwy, Dedham, MA 02026	781-326-5385

MISSOURI
9804 Watson Road, St. Louis, MO 63126	314-965-3512

NEW JERSEY
561 U.S. Route 1, Wick Plaza, Edison, NJ 08817	732-572-1200

NEW YORK
150 East 52nd Street, New York, NY 10022	212-754-1110

PENNSYLVANIA
9171-A Roosevelt Blvd, Philadelphia, PA 19114	215-676-9494

SOUTH CAROLINA
243 King Street, Charleston, SC 29401	843-577-0175

TENNESSEE
4811 Poplar Avenue, Memphis, TN 38117	901-761-2987

TEXAS
114 Main Plaza, San Antonio, TX 78205	210-224-8101

VIRGINIA
1025 King Street, Alexandria, VA 22314	703-549-3806

CANADA
3022 Dufferin Street, Toronto, ON M6B 3T5	416-781-9131

¡También somos su fuente para libros,
videos y música en español!